Fate Presents

WEREWOLVES AND DOGMEN

A werewolf attacks a man, from a 1517 woodcut.

Fate Presents

WEREWOLVES AND DOGMEN

Compiled and edited by

Rosemary Ellen Guiley

Visionary Living, Inc.
New Milford, Connecticut

FATE Presents Werewolves and Dogmen

Compiled and edited by Rosemary Ellen Guiley

Front cover design by April Slaughter
Back cover and interior design by Leslie McAllister

ISBN: 978-1-942157-17-5 (pbk)
ISBN: 978-1-942157-18-2 (epub)

Published by Visionary Living, Inc.
New Milford, Connecticut
www.visionaryliving.com

TABLE OF CONTENTS

ACKNOWLEDGMENTS

My thanks to Phyllis Galde, owner, publisher, and editor-in-chief of FATE magazine, for making this anthology, the first of a series, possible, and to the writers of the articles.

Special thanks go to Brian and Terrie Seech, founders of the Center for Cryptoozologial Studies, for their archival research assistance.

Preface

Since 1948, FATE magazine has kept its finger on the pulse of the paranormal: all the mysteries of land, sky, and the twilight places in between. The best researchers and writers in the field have been showcased in FATE, delivering to readers an astonishing range of articles probing the unknown.

The fascination with werewolves and their kin – dogmen and were-beasts – dates to ancient times. Werewolves have become a staple of supernatural lore, and, in modern times, a staple of horror entertainment as well. In entertainment, the beast is confined largely to the shapeshifting human who becomes a bloodthirsty monster, especially at the full moon, and possessing frightening supernatural powers.

The werewolf is much more than a monster, however; it has a mystery that reaches into the dark depths of the Unknown. The 32 articles in this superb collection reveal little-known aspects of the werewolf – and some of the true accounts are bone-chilling. Werewolves are not a thing of the past, not a flight of fancy, but real entities that still haunt the earth.

I have grouped articles together under themes:

- "Werewolves and Lycanthropes" includes lore, history, characteristics, and famous cases.
- "Werewolves in the Modern World" features real and creepy true accounts of present-day werewolves.
- "Dogmen and the Beast of Bray Road" concerns a relative of the werewolf, the wolf-human hybrid mystery creature.
- "Shapeshifters and Thoughtforms" delves into astral werewolves, psychic projections, magical forms, and connections to sorcery and witchcraft.

- "Spectral and Demon Dogs" features another werewolf cousin, the phantom black dog or hell hound that roams the planet, sometimes bringing bad luck and death.
- An appendix, "A Gazeteer of Werewolves," describes creatures from myth and lore around the world.

There is some overlap among the sections, and among the articles themselves. Each article nonetheless reveals something different and makes a unique contribution to werewolf lore. I have also included articles of my own. The entire collection is international, historical, and supernatural in scope. A few of the articles have no author bio information.

Some of the illustrations are taken directly from the pages of original issues, and some include the original captions as well.

I have included a brief history of FATE at the end. FATE still publishes issues, now in both hard print and electronic formats, and you can subscribe and become part of the FATE family.

I know you will enjoy exploring the mystery of werewolves. The next time you are out in some lonely place on a full moonlit night, you will always wonder.... what lurks out there in the darkness.

—Rosemary Ellen Guiley, executive editor, FATE

Introduction
An Overview of Werewolves and Their Kin
Rosemary Ellen Guiley

Werewolves have instilled fear and dread in human beings since ancient times. The wolf is one of the fiercest, most dangerous, and most cunning of animals. Combine it with the intelligence of a human, and the resulting creature becomes even more formidable. Add supernatural characteristics, and it becomes one of the supreme mystery beings.

Werewolves have long associations with witches, demons, vampires, spectral black dogs, dogmen, and other residents of the netherworld. Numerous cases have been documented around the world of ravening werewolves who went on bloody rampages, killing humans and beasts alike. In modern times, we seldom hear of the rampaging werewolf – but cases of predatory, killer werewolves still exist, usually in rural areas where the lore is strong. Werewolves have not gone away – they are still among us. They live in the shadows and prowl with stealth.

By definition, a werewolf is a human being who turns into a wolf and later resumes human form. During their episodes as wolves, werewolves savagely attack, kill and devour animals and people. The time spent in wolf form may be short, just as a few hours, or long, even years in cases attributed to curses.

Werewolfism has always had dark and demonic associations. The word "werewolf," or "man-wolf," was first recorded in Old English in the 11th century in the Ecclesiastical Ordinances of King Cnut (1017-1037), as a synonym for the devil. It was sometimes used to refer to outlaws.

Werewolves have also been called "lycanthropes." The term "lycanthropy" comes from *lycanthrope*, the Greek term for "man-wolf," which in turn was derived from the name of King Lycaon ("deluding wolf") of Greek mythology. Lycaon was turned into a wolf as divine punishment.

The story of King Lycaon appears in different versions, among them Roman works such as Ovid's *Metamorphoses* and Vergil's *Georgics*. The myth may be related to a cannibalism practice that was part of the cult of Jupiter Lycaeus in Roman times. According to the cult, a person who ate human flesh was transformed into a wolf and spent eight to 10 years in the wild. The werewolf could then resume human form, but only if it consumed no more human flesh.

King Lycaon is changed into a wolf by Jupiter.

According to Ovid's Roman version, Jupiter, king off the gods, was upset over the murder of Julius Caesar and the increasing wickedness of the human race. He descended from Mount Olympus and took on the form of a man, roaming about to check the state of affairs. At nightfall, he entered the home of King Lycaon, an "inhospitable tyrant," and revealed himself as a god. The people bowed down to worship him, but Lycaon laughed at them. He proposed an infallible test to determine if Jupiter was god or man.

Lycaon intended to steal upon Jupiter and kill him while he was asleep. But first he took a hostage sent to him by the Molossian people and slit his throat. He cooked the man's limbs, boiling some and roasting some. He set the human flesh out on his banquet table for the god.

Enraged, Jupiter destroyed the household with avenging flames. Lycaon escaped into the countryside with his life, but not free of the wrath of Jupiter, who caused him to become a wolf:

> *There he uttered howling noises, and his attempts to speak were all in vain. His clothes changed into bristling hairs, his arms to legs, and he became a wolf. His own savage nature showed in his rabid jaws, and he now directed against the flocks his innate lust for killing. He had a mania, even yet, for shedding blood. But, though he was a wolf, he retained some traces of his original shape. The greyness of his hair was the same, his face showed the same violence, his eyes gleamed as before, and he presented the same picture of ferocity.*

Jupiter resolved to destroy the entire human race and replace them with an entirely new stock of men "of miraculous origin."

In another version of the myth, Lycaon's evil sons killed one brother, Nyctimus, and made a soup of him. They offered the soup to Jupiter, who had disguised himself as a poor laborer. Outraged, Jupiter killed the evil sons with a lightning bolt, restored Nyctimus to life, and turned Lycaon into a wolf. Lycaon suffered a ravenous thirst for blood and went out slaughtering flocks of animals.

The words "lycanthropia" and "lycanthropus" made their first appearance in the English language in 1584 in the anti-witch-hunting book *The Discoverie of Witchcraft* by Reginald Scot. During the Inquisition, lycanthropy and werewolfism were used almost interchangeably.

More recently, "lycanthropy" has evolved into the term "lycans" to describe modern werewolves, especially those in film and gaming.

CHARACTERISTICS OF WEREWOLVES

The transformation, or metamorphosis, from human to wolf is complete, so that the wolf appears to others as a wolf and not a human-wolf hybrid, or the oversized monsters featured in horror films. The human acquires all the wolf senses and abilities, but in many historical accounts retains human intellect and emotion.

In lore, there are two types of werewolves: involuntary and voluntary.

The *involuntary werewolf* is a person cursed, perhaps because of a sin. The curse might last a few years or a lifetime. For example, an Armenian folk belief holds that a sinful woman is condemned to be a werewolf for seven years. A demon appears to her and commands her to don a wolf skin. When she does so, she assumes the nature of a wolf, devouring her children and then strangers, wandering about at night to wreak havoc and returning to human form in the morning.

The *voluntary werewolf* is a person who may like to eat human flesh and acquires magical skills that enable transformation into wolf form at will. The transformation is accomplished in various ways:

- By completely disrobing
- By donning a girdle or belt made of wolf skin or human skin
- By rubbing the body with magical ointment
- By drinking rain water that has collected in a wolf's footprints
- By reciting magical incantations
- By being aided by the devil or his demons

Characteristics of both types the werewolf are:

- An insatiable desire for the raw flesh and blood of animals and humans
- Insatiable sexual lusts
- Wolfish behavior, such as howling and running about on all fours
- Savage attacks on animals and people
- Exhaustion after werewolf episodes

Werewolf beliefs have existed since antiquity. Early humans may have established strong bonds with wolves – from whom dogs evolved – and there is evidence of various animal cults, in which

A man changes into a werewolf.

humans acquired animal powers by donning their skins. The *berserkir* and *eigi einhamir* of Nordic and Icelandic lore are examples of such animal cults. Early humans may also have practiced cannibalism. In the earliest religions, gods and goddesses had animal attributes. In ancient Egypt, the images of gods were as were-animals: human bodies with animal heads.

Werewolf beliefs were particularly strong in parts of Europe where wolves were common and presented dangers. Superstitions and fears of wolves ran high in the Baltic regions (Livonia, Latvia and Lithuania), France, Germany, Switzerland and even parts of Spain. Plague epidemics that decimated local populations enabled wolves to flourish. As they lost natural prey to hunters, they turned to livestock, pets and even humans, though attacks on humans were rare. France was particularly plagued with wolf terrors, the greatest of which was the Beast of Gevaudan. In England, wolves were exterminated by the 16th century, and so fear of wolves – and consequently stories of werewolves – are nearly absent there.

WEREWOLVES AND THE MOON

The notion that werewolves transform *only* at the full moon is more fiction than fact. In earlier stories, legends, and even real cases of werewolves, the transformations were accomplished at will or by curse. Sometimes the moon was a factor, and often was not.

In general, the moon has always been associated with the dark forces of the supernatural and spirit realms, with baleful influences, negativity, and insanity.

Some cases of lyncanthropy have featured a lunar influence. One modern case was documented in 1975 in the *Canadian Psychiatric Association Journal*. The man, identified only as "Mr. W.," was a 37-year-old Appalachian farmer. Shortly after his discharge from the U.S. Navy, Mr. W. began to show little interest in his farm chores or any daily activities. He let his facial hair grow, making believe that it was fur. He slept in cemeteries, and occasionally he would lie down on highways in front of approaching traffic. He howled at the moon. Mr. W.'s own explanation for his erratic behavior was that he had been transformed into a werewolf.

He was admitted to a psychiatric hospital, where doctors found that he was suffering from a chronic brain syndrome of undetermined origin, resulting in chronic undifferentiated schizophrenia. But doctors also concluded that the occurrence of his psychosis during the full moon – his moon madness – remained unexplained on an organic level.

SILVER

Since ancient times, silver, associated with the moon, has been held to have protective powers against negative influences and everything evil. Its connection to werewolves – that silver bullets are necessary to kill the beasts – is tenuous in lore and more a product of fiction.

Silver remedies against werewolves are absent in ancient lore. There are mentions of silver in witch-hunting writings of the Inquisition. Perhaps the best-known references to the power of silver against werewolves can be traced to stories surrounding the famed Beast of Gevaudan, a giant, ravaging wolf that plagued France in the 18th century. The beast seemed invulnerable to bullets, but was finally shot to death. Later stories introduced the element that silver bullets had brought it down. From the 18th century onward, silver bullets became established "fact" as necessary to kill a werewolf.

WOLF'S BANE

Wolf's bane is a poisonous flowering plant, known as aconitum – one of hundreds in the aconite family – and is an ingredient in various old magical ointments. It is a narcotic and pain reliever, and causes hallucinations. It was said to be an ingredient in ointments used by witches for enabling them to fly. It was once administered to dying persons to speed and enhance the process of dying. It is highly toxic, and even touching the plant can cause severe reactions.

The Roman writer Ovid stated in *Metamorphoses* that wolf's bane is born from the slavering mouth of Cerberus, the triple-headed dog beast that guards the entrance to Hades. One of the effects of the aconitum poison causes a foaming mouth similar to a rabid animal. From there the connection can be made to a slavering werewolf.

In earlier times, wolf's bane was used to poison arrowheads in the hunting of wolves.

In fiction, it is portrayed as an antidote to the bite of a werewolf. In Bram Stoker's *Dracula*, wolf's bane is used as a protection against vampires. In the 1941 film *The Wolf Man*, the transformation from human to wolf occurs at the full moon in the fall when wolfbane blooms – a fiction. Characters in the film wear sprigs of wolf's bane to ward off the werewolf – a dangerous action given the toxicity of the plant.

In other fictional (and sometimes contradictory) lore, wolf's bane repels and even kills werewolves, but if it is smelled, worn, or eaten it will turn a person into a werewolf.

In in the *Ginger Snaps* films (2000-2004), dried monkshood, a plant related to wolf's bane, is administered to a person infected with werewolfism to inhibit their transformation to werewolf.

WEREWOLVES AND VAMPIRES

Werewolves have a strong connection to vampires. In Slavic lore, the werewolf is closely related to the vampire, and in some beliefs, one has the potential to become the other. The name of the Serbo-Croatian *vukodlak* vampire means "wolf's hair." *Vlokoslak*, a Serbian term, and *vrykolakas*, a Greek term, are among the names that are applied to either a vampire or a werewolf. Many European superstitions about vampires hold that they can shapeshift into various animal forms besides wolves.

WEREWOLVES AND WITCHCRAFT

In the 15th and 16th centuries, the Inquisition was at its peak. Stories of werewolves shifted to reports of bloodthirsty rampages, for which people were tried and executed. Werewolves, like witches, were seen as servants of the devil. In Europe people accused of shapeshifting and other acts of witchcraft were burned. In the Pyrenees alone, some 200 men and women "werewolves" were sent to their deaths.

Some demonologists accepted the concept of werewolf metamorphosis, but most believed it to be a delusional state of mind, perhaps even one created by the devil. King James I of England (King James VI of Scotland) wrote in his *Demonology* (1597) that werewolves, or "ManWoolfes," were not people under the influence of the devil, but suffered from delusions and melancholia, and imitated wolf behavior.

Some accused werewolves clearly were mentally unstable and deranged people. In 1541, a deranged farmer in Pavia who murdered several persons was arrested as a werewolf. One of his claims upheld a popular superstition, that werewolves have their wolf pelts on the inside of their human skins. To verify this, the authorities cut off all his limbs. They found no wolf pelt, of course. The accused, now innocent, unfortunately died several days later.

DOGMEN

Sightings of mysterious creatures that appear to be part human and part wolf are reported in modern times all over the world. They are often erroneously called "werewolves." Their apparent hybrid nature makes them "dogmen" or "man-wolves." One of the most famous is the Beast of Bray Road, a large creature seen in rural areas in Wisconsin and Michigan. The first known reported sighting occurred in 1936.

Reports of dogmen date to ancient times. In some cases, they were thought to be a type of debased human. The Cynocephali, or Dog-heads, were well known in classical times, and were among the

Dog-headed man from India.

most feared of monstrous races. They were described as fire-breathing cannibals with enormous teeth.

A race of raw-meat-eating dog-headed men said to live in India was described as early as the 4th century BCE. Ctesias of Cnidus, the court physician to Artaxerxes of Persia and a philosopher, historian, and writer, wrote of them. He was extensively quoted later by Pliny the Elder in the 1st century in his work *Historia Naturalis*. Ctesias gave this description of the "Dog-headed Men of the Northern Hills":

> *In the hills there are men who have a dog's head, and whose clothes are the skins of wild beasts. They have no language; they bark like dogs and so make themselves understood to one another. Their teeth are longer than those of dogs; their nails are like those of animals, but longer and more curved. They are black and very honest, like the rest of the Indians, with whom they trade; they*

understand the Indian language, but they cannot reply
except by barking and making signs with their hands and
fingers like deaf-mutes. The Indians call them Calystrians
in their language, which means dog-headed. They live on
raw meat. Their population may reach 129,000.

Ctesias never explained how he derived the population numbers.

Ctesias's writings have long been dismissed by scientists, who point out that he never went to India himself and knew about the dogmen only through hearsay and secondhand reports. Explanations that have been proposed are that the dogmen really were monkeys or a race of hairy pygmies called Vedduh from Ceylon.

The explorer Marco Polo (1254-1354) described a race of dogmen on the island of "Angaman," which may have been one of the Andaman Islands in the Bay of Bengal off the coast of India. Polo has also been dismissed as having been influenced by Ctesias.

In Egyptian lore, Queen Hatshepsut sent sailors to the "Island of Punt" (part of Somalia), where they said they found dog-headed men who were fierce warriors.

References to dog-headed men appear in Christian literature and lore. The Theodore Psalter, an illustrated manuscript dated 1066 in the British Library, features an illustration of Jesus preaching to dog-headed men; they might have symbolized the primitive heathen. An apochryphal work, The Contendings of the Apostles, Ethiopic texts translated into English in 1899, tells of Andrew and Bartholomew preaching to a giant cannibal named Abominable, who had a doglike head and bestial body features. And, the legendary St. Christopher was described in the 8th century as being "one of the Dog-heads" who ate human flesh.

In North America, the Dogmen of Michigan roam the northern part of the state, and have been extensively researched by Linda S. Godfrey. Their legends date to the 19th century, when loggers reported an encounter with a strange, large black dog that reared up on its hind legs.

Folklore accounts recorded since then tell of sightings of creatures with dog heads and man bodies. The dogmen were said to break into houses and buildings, leaving claw and teeth marks on doors, and to attack people and animals, some of whom supposedly died of fright. A creature with a man's body and a dog's head was seen swimming in Claybank Lake near Manistee, where fishermen said they had to fight it off to keep it out of their boat.

Some modern researchers believe dogmen are real and physical residents of the planet, however, perhaps prehistoric hold-overs. Others believe them to be residents of parallel dimensions who somehow find their way into the human world. If so, these entities would not be werewolves or were-animals in the classic sense of a transformed human, but may be weird hybrids existing in their natural state.

Whatever the explanation, the physical evidence for them is rare. Researchers collect casts of unusual footprints and collect hair and dung samples that sometimes are found to be of "unknown" origin, but no conclusive physical proof has yet been found that such creatures exist – at least in corporeal reality.

SHAPESHIFTERS

Certain human beings are credited with the ability to shapeshift into animal forms, including weredogs. This shapeshifting ability is called "cyanthropy," which derives from "cyanthrope," or "man-dog."

Werewolf.

A Native American legend tells about weredogs who became tribal ancestors. According to the story, an Indian took up residence along the shores of the Great Bear lake. He had a female dog who was pregnant. It gave birth to eight puppies. Whenever the Indian man went out to fish, he tied up the puppies in his tent to prevent them from straying. Upon his return, he would hear childish laughter and talking coming from his tent, but when he entered it, he would find only the puppies.

One day he pretended to go away to fish, but hid near the tent. When he heard the children's voices, he rushed into the tent and found beautiful children there laughing and playing. They had dog-skins by their sides.

He took the dog-skins and threw them on the fire. The children were stuck in their human form, and they became the ancestors of the dog-rib nation.

Magically skilled individuals also know how to shapeshift into animal forms. Shamanic traditions hold that certain empowered sorcerers can shapeshift into animal and hybrid forms, including the wolf. For example, in Mexico, the *nahual* is a type of shapeshifted sorcerer. The term "nahual" derives from "nahualli," an Aztec term meaning "sorcerer" or "warlock." The favored form of the *nahual* is a large coyote.

According to lore, the sorcerer uses black magic to shapeshift. Methods include going into a trance or deep sleep (which suggest an emergence into an astral form); jumping over a wooden cross; and using herbs and ointments which probably contain hallucinogenic ingredients. Some sorcerers are said to be born with ability to shapeshift at will.

Once transformed, it wreaks evil and destruction upon people in its animal form. It steals and eats both livestock and crops, and will attack humans as well. The *nahual* will fight other shapeshifters who threaten their territory. Like the European werewolf, a wounded *nahual* will show the same wound when it reverts to human form.

The *nahual* can be killed by shooting, stoning, hanging, and being doused with holy water; the latter is a Christianized element introduced after the conquests of the Spaniards spread Christian practices and beliefs.

In the Southwestern United States, Native American sorcerer shapeshifters are called "skinwalkers."

THERIANTHROPY

Therianthropy is the metamorphosis or transformation of humans into animal forms, and has come into popular usage in modern times among individuals in the living vampire and living werewolf subcultures. A "therian" is someone who identifies with an animal form and spirit and interacts with it in various ways, for example, as a tutelary or totem spirit; in shamanic or astral journeys; and in taking on the animal form in some way. Some therians say they can shapeshift their bodies to take on real animal characteristics to different degrees, such as wolf's hair and claws. However, none volunteer themselves to science for study.

Therians intermingle in the living vampire communities or have their own organizations. Some call themselves "lycans" after fictional characters.

MEDICAL LYCANTHROPY

Today, outside of entertainment, the term "lycanthropy" is used to describe a clinical disorder in which a person believes himself to be transformed into a wolf, and acts accordingly. Lycanthropy is linked to schizophrenia, multiple personality disorder, bipolar disorder, drug abuse, clinical vampirism, mental retardation, necrophilia, and other psychological disorders.

The dominant features of lycanthropic behavior are:

- Profound alienation from self and society
- Obsession with things demonic
- Frequenting of cemeteries and other lonely places
- A secret process or ritual of supposed transformation from human form to wolf form
- Belief that one actually grows fur, fangs, paws, etc.
- An insatiable lust for blood
- Wolf-life behavior, including howling, running on all fours, gnawing objects, attacking people and animals with the intent to kill, biting and tearing at flesh, and the devouring of raw flesh, including human
- Hyper sexual activity, including bestiality

- Supposed resumption of human form
- Post-exhaustion, confusion and depression
- Impaired mental functioning

Lycanthropy has been recognized as a medical disorder since the 2nd century. The Greek physician Galen (born c. 130) considered it to be a melancholic disease with delirium. The Roman Marcellus of Side (c. 161) described its symptoms. The Greek physician Paul of Aegina (625-690), who based his writings on those of Marcellus, was the first to link lycanthropy to melancholia. The symptoms of lycanthropes reported by Paul are:

> *...they are pale, their vision feeble, their eyes dry, tongue very dry, and the flow of the saliva stopped; but they are thirsty, and their legs have incurable ulcerations from frequent falls.*

The prescribed remedies of ancient times were a form of medical exorcism aimed at driving the affliction out of the body: massive bloodletting to the point of fainting, a diet of "wholesome food" and baths of sweet water and milk-whey. The patient was purged with various agents, including toxic herbs. Rubbing the nostrils with opium prior to sleep also was prescribed – a remedy that probably exacerbated the condition rather than alleviated it.

During the Inquisition, lycanthropy was linked to demonic influences. Most demonologists considered it to be an illusion, the product of insanity or disease caused by the devil. Some believed that people made actual transformations into wolves with the help of demons. Coinciding with the witch hunts were regional hysterias over wolves that ravaged the countryside, killing people and animals. Many peasants believed man-eating wolves to be werewolves. Some high-profile werewolf trials involved confessions of witchcraft as well as lycanthropy. Descriptions of some of the accused reveal them to be probable sufferers of the medical disorder.

Some authorities of the 16th and 17th centuries considered lycanthropy to be madness alone, without the aid of enchantment or the devil. Among those of this opinion were Reginald Scot, the demonologist Johann Weyer, the French physician Jean Nynauld and the Oxford cleric Robert Burton.

After the end of the Inquisition, lycanthropy was considered madness, insanity, hysteria melancholy, and delusion well into the 19th century. With the emergence of the field of psychology, lycanthropy nearly disappeared from medical literature. Between 1873 and 1975, only one case was mentioned. Carl G. Jung briefly referred to a case resembling lycanthropy (or zoanthropy, referring to animals in general) in 1928 in an essay on how children are sensitive to the unconscious dynamics of their parents. In that case, the mother suffered insanity and would crawl around on all fours grunting like a pig, barking like a dog and growling like a bear. The children had nightmares of her as a witch or dangerous animal.

In the mid-1970s, cases of lycanthropy and zoanthropy were recorded in medical literature, along with an increase in diagnoses of multiple personality disorders. It is doubtful that lycanthropy disappeared, but probably was diagnosed as another condition, such as paranoia or hysteria.

In psychology, lycanthropy may be related to the "beast within," a dissociated part of the psyche that separates humans from baser instincts and animalistic behavior. In Jungian terms, this is part of the shadow, a hidden, primitive and repressed personality that may go back to humanity's earliest ancestors. In cases of lycanthropy, this hidden side finds expression.

Treatment for lycanthropy includes antidepressants, neuroleptics and other medications, and psychotherapy. Some patients experience partial or complete remission.

The articles in this book explore all aspects of werewolves, dogmen, and their cousins the spectral black dogs. Some of the cases are famous. Some will shock you. And some will make you think twice about the reality of the werewolf.

WEREWOLVES AND LYCANTHROPES

A CASE FOR WEREWOLVES
Scott Corrales

Lycanthropy, with all of its variations, is one of the areas of high strangeness which persistently reappear, year after year, in newspaper clippings and magazines, and present evidence of having been visited by many authors in dusty old books found at garage sales and church basements.

It is a fascination that binds the anthropologist, the folklorist, and the paranormalist in a Gordian knot that is hard to slice with the toughest research tools. It haunted man in the caves, haunted religion in the Middle Ages, haunted the silver screen during the 20th century, and reared its ugly, hairy head even in the 1990s. This article will examine some of its aspects in the hope of adding another mite of esoteric lore to the existing stockpile.

From prehistory to the present
Every single one of the Western European languages has a word to describe the human who, by means sorcerous or otherwise, effects the

transformation into a wolf (or other creature, as we shall see later) to commit heinous crimes around its locality. English gives us *werewolf*, literally "man-wolf" in Old English; French gives us *loup-garou*; Spanish gives us *hombre lobo*; Italian renders it as *lupo manaro;* and Portuguese surprises us with two variations: *lob omem* and *lobizón*.

The name game is interesting but offers little by way of information. What happens in places where there are no wolves and never have been any? The local lore then accepts that humans are able to shed their skins and assume the shape of other animals, such as the Mexican *nagual*, which assumes the shape of a dog or fox. African animism accepted the possibility of sorcerers shapeshifting into hyenas or even leopards; Chinese and Japanese legend features the werefox and the werevixen, who could take human form and mate with humans. Far from being feared and loathed, the werevixen was considered to be highly desirable because of its skills in the art of love.

Anthropologists assuage our fears by telling us that the belief in werewolves (or other werecreatures) is a throwback to primitive man's rituals in the caves of Western Europe, where shamans would don the skins of a totemic animal (bears, wolves, deer) and lead lodges of initiates – usually young tribesmen being inducted into the ranks of a warrior/hunter class-in frenzied dances. The hunter, aided perhaps by an intoxicant substance, visualized himself as the predator, acquiring its stealth, strength, and sagacity. (A *Time/Life* book entitled *The Epic of Man* depicts such rituals in intricate detail.)

But something strange happened on the way from the caves.

Tribes evolved into clans, then city-states, and finally nations. Millennia-old rites were forgotten and replaced with elaborate ritual. Although no one invoked the protection of the wolf, the bear, or other such totemic forces anymore, there remained the very real fear of people who were actually able to become such animals – not to pursue prey, but to terrorize their fellow men.

Medieval Christian authorities held as an irrefutable fact that lycanthropy was only possible if the human desiring said capacity requested it directly from the devil. This belief was later extended to include what we nowadays might call "no-fault" lycanthropes: hapless children conceived during the new moon, those who may have unwittingly drunk out of a watering hole frequented by wolves or eaten of the flesh of a lamb slain by a wolf; and other gems of medieval thought. Scandinavians believed in *berserkir*, warriors who were able to assume animal shapes – bears and wolves in particular. In the heat of battle, and literally driven berserk, these warriors slavered at the mouth like wolves or growled like bears. There are always bits of lore of armored combatants becoming aware of a huge bear fighting in their midst – the berserker in action.

Slightly more sophisticated is the belief that certain humans could project their souls into animals or else construct animal shapes for themselves. Chroniclers disagreed if a physical change into an animal actually took place, or if the minds of observers were clouded into seeing the human as a wolf or other creature.

In parts of equatorial Africa, there was a firmly held belief that the souls of departed chieftains would enter the bodies of lions and roam the night. Said necromantic versions of the Lion King were known as *Pondoro* and were greatly feared and respected.

A gathering of werewolves, by Maurice Sand, 1858.

Sorcery and shapeshifting go hand in claw. Witches were thought to have acquired the loathsome ability as part of their pacts with the devil, causing nocturnal terror in their communities for a given period of time. *The History of the Goths, Swedes and Vandals*, by the medieval chronicler Olaus Magnus, states that the losses caused by wolves were not nearly so great as those produced by werewolves. Latvian tales report a Christmastime depredation of thousands of wolves, allegedly led by the devil himself under the guise of a great wolf. This unholy host engaged in concerted attacks upon humans and their livestock for the duration of the 12 days of Christmas, when the werewolves would suddenly find themselves returned to human form. While this bit of folklore may sound familiar to readers of J. R. R. Tolkien's *Silmarillion*, in which the evil Sauron assumes the form of a werewolf, the concept of wolf packs in the thousands headed by demons is widespread, and persists to this very day.

In October 1996, a curious news story was circulated by the Reuters World Service. Elements of the Egyptian police had allegedly shot and captured two strange, savage animals of a pack that had terrorized the small Egyptian town of Armant, a community in the Nile Valley some 300 miles south of Cairo, killing three villagers and wounding dozens in a series of nocturnal raids against the population.

The news item went on to say that the bloodthirsty creatures resembled "large hyenas or wild dogs." Known to the locals as *salaawwa*, the beasts allegedly belonged to no known species of canids. Egypt's Ministry of the Interior offered the theory that the animals had been driven northward from the Sudan in search of new hunting grounds. Armed villagers joined the gendarmes in efforts to ensnare the bizarre animals, ultimately managing to wound a specimen as it emerged from the farmland bent on attacking individual homes. Another such creature had been shot dead, and no further information was available on the beasts.

In a world in which new species are added to the roster every year, the news of hyena offshoots attacking humans in the Nile should simply be chalked up to animal reactions resulting from changes in the environment. But the Egyptian news story has a curious ring of familiarity to it.

In the year A.D. 774, during the reign of Emperor Leo IV, called "the Khazar," the Eastern Roman Empire was swept by a plague of quasi-biblical proportions, followed by the appearance of bizarre carnivorous animals who could be dead ringers for the one in the Reuters item. A Syriac priest and chronicler of the time, Denys de Tell-Mahre, describes the creatures as having no fear of humans and resembling wolves, but with smaller, narrower muzzles and horse-like ears. "The skin on their dorsal spine resembled the bristles of pigs," he adds.

Swarms of these strange canids fanned out across Anatolia, devouring dozens of farmers and villagers. The animals fought their human attackers fiercely, unafraid of weapons, brazenly carrying off children out of homes and fields.

Soon, however, we begin to encounter clearly paranormal overtones emerging from this Syriac chronicle: the nameless beasts were able to "abduct children from their beds," and dogs refused to bark at their appearance. Entire herds of cattle were destroyed, and "when one of them attacked a herd of goats, or flock of sheep, it took away several at a time," adds the chronicle.

Native American traditions feature werecreatures as a prominent part of their religious beliefs. In the Southwest, the Navajo believed in "skinwalkers" – individuals who, like their Mexican counterparts farther south, use this talent (or curse) for evil purposes. The Navajo term for these practitioners of the black arts translates as "those who walk around with a wolf skin."

Werewolfery examined

The concept of lycanthropy harkens back to the Greek myth of King Lycaeon of Arcadia, who was turned into a wolf by a wrathful Zeus after the hapless monarch sacrificed a child to propitiate the unpredictable deity. Only slightly less mythical are the physical transformations allegedly experienced by mighty Nebuchadnezzar of Babylon, who ran the gamut of werewolf experiences ranging from nocturnal escapades to violent attacks on his subjects.

German tradition gives us the frightening tale of Sigmund and Sinfjotli, who came upon a cabin in the woods whose occupants were afflicted by a terrible curse: they could only recover their human appearance every 10 days. Moved by curiosity, the two heroes donned wolf-skin cloaks they found in the abode and within hours turned into wolfmen – horrified at their animal countenances, which endured for 10 days. Once the spell relented, Sigmund and Sinfjotli torched the wolf cloaks, bringing the curse to an end.

The vast majority of these ancient claims of men turning into beasts can be explained as outbreaks of zoanthropy, the disease that makes certain mental patients imagine themselves as having turned into animals. Medical researchers in the 19th century managed to explain how schizophrenia and epilepsy played a major role in this pathology. A less-than-stable mind would turn simple nocturnal dream activity into authentic experiences.

Cases of hypertrichosis – the birth of children completely covered with facial and bodily hair – certainly must have contributed to the widespread belief in werewolves. In the 17th century, Pedro Gonzalez, a Spanish nobleman from the Canary Islands, was afflicted with this condition and was forced to leave his sunny isles for what is now Switzerland. The condition reached public awareness when in 1986, the story of the Mexican "wolf boys" hit the media, involving three brothers suffering from hypertrichosis. Certainly, there are places on earth where such "wolf children" are venerated, as was the case with Sher Ali Shah, who was discovered in Bangladesh in 1990 and whose condition is considered supernatural in origin.

Such is the case of such famous "were-wolves" as Jacques Roulet, a 16th-century Frenchman from the locality of Angiers, who was found naked and bloody-handed in the forests of Western France by a group of peasants. The situation was understandably worsened by the discovery of the mangled corpse of a young man not far away.

In August 1598, judge Pierre Herault presided over the werewolf's trial. Athough the latter had been declared unfit to stand trial, he nonetheless spoke freely of the crime and of a "strange ointment" that caused his hands to turn into wolf claws. The case against Roulet was unanimous and the death sentence was called for, but the defendant successfully appealed to the Parisian Parliament, thus commuting the order of execution for two years in an insane asylum at St. Germain-des-Pres.

Perhaps the French justice system was Cartesian even back in the late 1500s, but elsewhere in Europe, Roulet would have met a more tragic fate at the hands of the Inquisition. Books compiled by demonologists such as Pierre de Lancre meticulously described the means by which men turned into wolves during the full moon, only to regain human shape at daybreak by rolling in mud or morning dew. Such tracts prescribed the use of silver bullets (due to that metal's association with the moon) and the burning of the lycanthrope's body just to be sure.

A werewolf attacks a woman, from a 19th-century French woodcut.

In spite of all the misinterpretation over the ages, do we have any cases that prove conclusively (whatever *that* means in the world of the paranormal!) that werewolves existed at any point in human history? Aside from cases of *nagualismo* in Mexico and isolated reports of bona-fide shapeshifting, the amount of evidence is small. However, when we examine the possibility of vulpine creatures of a strictly nonhuman nature, the situation changes radically.

Reports persist down to our decade of what appear to be manlike animals able to walk on two legs and who meet the criteria used centuries ago to describe werewolves. Whether these entities are manifestations of archetypal images (as suggested by Dr. Greg Little in his masterful *People of the Web*), projections of the collective unconscious, consciously-created *tulpas* as described by Tibet scholar Alexandra David-Neel, denizens from a dimension bordering our own, or simply hell spawn, the cases and the events they describe are nothing if not compelling.

Some contemporary cases

In 1993, Wisconsin journalist Linda S. Godfrey published a pair of articles in *Strange Magazine* concerning the "Bray Road Beast." These reports described a series of multiple-witness encounters with a lupine entity haunting Walworth County, Wisconsin, between 1989 and 1990.

The initial 1989 sighting was made by Lori Endrizzi, who reported "a kneeling creature with glowing eyes that stared at her as it held road kill in its claws." Subsequent witnesses to the same entity believed they were seeing a dog, until it stood up on its hind legs before dropping back down and giving chase to the onlookers. One witness claimed that the Beast had run toward her car and landed on its trunk just before she managed to speed off.

In July 1993, *Paradigmas* magazine presented curious reports from Latin America that hinted at a sudden outbreak of lycanthropy. Residents of the town of Rivera, north of the Uruguayan capital of Montevideo, were terrified that a supposedly "mythical" creature had been instrumental in attacks upon two young women. The first victim was attacked at night as she returned home from work. The wolf-creature, denominated *lobizón* by the locals, tore her dress and ran its claws across her chest, leaving deep claw marks. The second victim, who chose to remain anonymous in the face of the "deep shame" she experienced, was apparently sexually assaulted by the *lobizón*.

Local police officials denied the existence of any supernatural creature, and went as far as to cast doubt upon the injured victims' suffering. The eldest residents of the area, however, made the sign of the cross whenever the subject was broached and even recited a number of prayers whose purpose was to ward off the evil creature.

The lycanthrope shifted its activities northward and re-emerged two years later near the community of Tres Lagos (Matto Grosso do Sul), where on March 14, 1995, at 1:30 in the morning, it staged an attack upon Wilson Dourado de Paula, a well-known soccer player, as the man left a family reunion. Dourado de Paula reported that the creature was six-and-a-half feet tall, and entirely black in color, with fiery red eyes and a pointed tail. The soccer star fended the giant entity off with a stone, after it very nearly succeeded in seizing him. Witnesses to the event were Anibal Jose Pedro and Dirceu Arruda.

While no further attacks upon humans were reported, evidence of the creature appeared a year later in Sao Roque (Sao Paulo) on October 7, 1996. Eduardo Roberto de Moraes, a local farmer, came across a number of claw-shaped footprints deeply etched into dry, hardened soil. Some of the prints in question measured up to 13 inches in length. On a local fence were found tufts of brownish-gray hair, presumed to be that of the creature. Analysis of the footprints led to the belief that the creature weighed some 440 pounds. According to the testimony of two witnesses who encountered the creature, it resembled a dog standing some five feet tall, with large black eyes, long fangs, and a body entirely covered in dense yellow fur. A mane of sorts ran down its back. The entity was able to walk grotesquely on its two hind legs or on all fours. Brazilian UFO researcher Encarnacion Zapata Garcia submitted the hair samples to the University of Sao Paulo to have them analyzed.

Meanwhile, on the opposite side of the world, the Indian subcontinent was experiencing the depredations of what many considered either a pack of roving werewolves – or Pakistanis in wolves' clothing.

According to an item in the *New York Times International* dated September 1, 1996, Anand Kumar, a four-year-old from the village of Banbirbur, was seized from the midst of a gathering of family members by a wolf which, when standing, "... was as tall as a man," according to one of the witnesses. To confuse matters further, the "wolf" was described as wearing a dark coat and goggles, making the case either a landmark of garbled translation or one of high strangeness.

Scott Corrales: A frequent contributor to FATE, *and the editor of* lnexplicata: The Journal of Hispanic Ufology.

FATE October 2000

WEREWOLVES
Gordon Stein

Few people today would admit to belief in werewolves. But not all that long ago – no more than one or two centuries ago – such creatures were widely assumed to be real and authorities documented a number of cases of werewolfery.

What is a werewolf? Perhaps the simplest way in which we can define one is by what it does. Here is a verbatim description (with modern spelling) of what Olaus Magnus said about werewolves in the English version of his *A Compendious History of the Goths, Swedes, and Other Northern Nations* (1658):

> In the feast of Christ's nativity, in the night, at a certain place, that they are resolved amongst themselves, there is gathered such a huge multitude of wolves changed from men that dwell in diverse places, which afterwards the same night doth to rage with a wonderful fierceness, both against mankind and other creatures, that are not fierce

by nature, that the inhabitants of that country suffer more hurt from them than ever they do from natural wolves. For, as it is proved, they set upon the houses of men that are in the woods with a wonderful fierceness, and labor to break down the doors, whereby they may destroy both men and other creatures that remain there. They get into beer cellars, and there they drink out some tuns of beer or mead, and they heap all the empty vessels one upon the other in the midst of the cellar, and so they leave them, wherein they differ from natural and true wolves.

Presumably natural and true wolves pile their empties up neatly.

In the Middle Ages werewolves were the subject of learned treatises which examined the phenomenon of "lycanthropy," as the condition of being a werewolf is called. The hotbed of werewolf activity seems to have been France and the peak period of persecutions for werewolfery was in the 1500s and 1600s. One of the more famous cases of this period was that of Jean Grenier. In 1603 three girls were tending their sheep in a village in southwest France when a strange-looking 14-year-old boy, Jean Grenier, came by and told them that he was a werewolf. He said that a man "gave me a wolf-skin cape; he wraps it around me and every Monday, Friday and Sunday, for about an hour at dusk, I am a wolf, a werewolf. I have killed dogs and drunk their blood; but little girls taste better and their flesh is tender and sweet, their blood rich and warm."

Today this sort of display would be dismissed as adolescent boasting and an attempt to scare the girls. But several children had been killed in a nearby region and so authorities took seriously the testimony of the three girls. Grenier was arrested.

Jean's father testified at his trial that Jean was an "idiot" (i.e., mentally deficient). All of Jean's stories were checked for accuracy. His house was searched in an attempt to find the magic ointment which he claimed he rubbed on himself to change into a wolf. No ointment was found. Jean, however, proved his own worst enemy. The boy insisted so vehemently that his story was true that even in the absence of supporting evidence the court convicted him. He was sentenced to be hanged and his body burned to ashes. The Parlement of Bordeaux decided to review the case. It brought in two physicians to examine

Jean. The physicians concluded that he was suffering from lycanthropy, the "disease" of werewolfery. Jean was condemned to be imprisoned for life in a local monastery. His mental condition seems to have further deteriorated in confinement and he died seven years later, purportedly now "a good Christian."

Only a few years earlier, in 1598, another French court tried a poor beggar named Jacques Roulet on a charge of being a werewolf. Roulet had been hiding half-naked in some bushes, with his face and hands covered with blood and gore. Nearby was the mutilated body of a 15-year-old boy. Roulet confessed to killing the boy but he claimed that it had happened after he rubbed himself with ointment obtained from his parents. Roulet said the ointment made him become a wolf, although whether he meant mentally or physically is not clear from his testimony.

A werewolf carries off a child.

The court sentenced him to death but he appealed to the Parlement of Paris and his sentence was changed to two years' imprisonment in an insane asylum, with instruction in religion. There is no record of what happened to him after this.

How did the idea that a man can turn into an animal arise? And why into a wolf?

The man-into-wolf motif, known all over the world, has sparked much scholarly controversy. This much, at least, seems clear: The earliest manifestation of the man-wolf conversion was probably the simple donning of a wolf skin or wolf robe for protection from the cold.

Subsequently people came to believe that the powers of the wolf would pass to the man wearing the skin. This "magical" aspect is an important ingredient in such other uses of the wolf skin as a disguise when spying, exacting vengeance on others or simply appearing to have power over others.

Human beings could also change into a number of other "were-animals." "Were" apparently means "man," so a werewolf is a man-wolf. But there are also were-bears, were-tigers, were-hyenas, were-lions, were-crocodiles and were-jackals. We should not forget that vampires are a form of were-bat. The idea that a human being can turn into an animal is a folk belief of worldwide distribution. In many cases the fiercest animal indigenous to a particular region is the one that will be chosen in the area's folklore as a were-animal. For example, an area that has no wolves but does have tigers will have stories about were-tigers but not werewolves.

In modern times no one, so far as I can determine, has been caught and accused of werewolfery, even though a few killings of animals have been attributed to werewolves. Nonetheless today's werewolf has flourished as a fixture in movies and fantastic fiction.

The earliest important mention of a werewolf in fiction may be the 12th-century poem known in English as *William of Palerne*, or the *Romance of William and the Werwolf*. But the werewolf theme was seldom used in literature before the 19th century. The first definitive werewolf story in English seems to be "Hugues, the Wer-Wolf," by Sutherland Menzies, published in a British magazine in 1838.

An early novel with a werewolf theme was Alexandre Dumas' *Le Meneur de Loups* (The Wolf Leader), published in 1857. Robert Louis Stevenson's *Dr. Jekyll and Mr. Hyde* (1886) contains many elements of werewolfery. Among other modern examples are Eden Phillpotts' 1899 short-story collection *Loup-Garou!* (French for werewolf) and Guy Endore's *The Werewolf of Paris* (1933). In recent years novels such as Gary Brandner's *The Howling* (1977) and Whitley Strieber's *The Wolfen* (1979) have been widely read.

The Endore, Brandner and Strieber novels were all made into films (the movie version of Endore's was called *Curse of the Werewolf*

(1961). The earliest werewolf film was the 1913 Bison release *The Werewolf*. In 1935 Universal produced *Werewolf of London* but the most famous werewolf film of all, Universal's *The Wolf Man* starring Lon Chaney, Jr., did not appear until six years later. Although it contains a bit of authentic werewolf lore, most of the time accuracy has been sacrificed for dramatic effect. In 1943 a sequel, *Frankenstein Meets the Wolf Man*, starred Lon Chaney and Bela Lugosi. Werewolves appeared in *House of Frankenstein* (1944), *House of Dracula* (1945) and *Abbott and Costello Meet Frankenstein* (1948). The next generation of werewolf movies was designed for teenagers: *I Was a Teenage Werewolf* (1957), *Werewolf in a Girls' Dormitory* (1961) and *Werewolf on Wheels* (1971).

Psychiatric explanations for werewolfery have ranged from psychosis to drug-induced states to the reappearance of some deeply buried racial memories on the part of an agricultural creature (man) who was forced to become a hunter. In fact, this last is the theme of the book *Man into Wolf* (1951) in which author Robert Eisler invokes a Jungian interpretation to try to explain werewolfery. How successful he is has a lot to do with whether you accept Jung's ideas in the first place. If you do, you may like Eisler's idea that in the collective unconscious of the human race there is a behavior pattern that goes back to the days when men were forced by changing climatic conditions to abandon their peaceful agricultural existence and become hunter-killers. When wild archetypal dreams from this period break into consciousness, a person may commit violent, animalistic acts, typical of what we know of lycanthropic behavior. Eisler's book consists of 52 pages of text, backed up by 219 pages of notes. He tries hard to document his case but I think his premises are dubious.

According to more traditional psychiatric explanations, the imagined transformation into a wolf is a way of experiencing relief from conflicts that might have led to suicide. Or it may result from paranoid schizophrenia (sometimes coupled with drug use) or from mental deficiency coupled with brain damage. In fact, there is not a great deal of psychiatric writing on the subject of werewolfery. The only common threads in the few reported cases examined by psychiatrists have been depersonalization and heavy use of psychotropic drugs.

I have already mentioned that belladonna can produce hallucinations that somewhat resemble those described by persons claiming to be werewolves. The drug stramonium (from the jimson weed) has toxic properties similar to belladonna, to which its active ingredients are closely related. Other related substances (all belladonna-like alkaloids) can be found in nightshade, henbane and aconite. All have been reported many times as the ingredients in both werewolf and witch's salves. All of these substances are hallucinogenic. They also produce dry mouth, restlessness, delirium and, on occasion, toxic psychosis (all reported among users of the salve). The toxic effects on the central nervous system may last 48 hours.

So, is werewolfery simply the result of a drug overdose? I don't think so. Yes, drug effects have played a role in some cases. It seems unlikely, however, that any one explanation will suffice to explain all reported cases of lycanthropy. No doubt some people who claimed to be werewolves were suffering from the effects of potent hallucinatory drugs. Some were psychotic. Some may have been suffering from the effects of a psychological contagion, perhaps combined with mass poisoning by ergot.

Ergot, a fungus occasionally found on grain, contains chemicals similar to LSD. In France and England there have been several documented outbreaks of ergot poisoning during which large numbers of people in the affected areas barked and howled like wolves and foamed at the mouth. The last major outbreak occurred in Devonshire, England, in 1700.

Finally, it has been suggested that lycanthropy is really only a medical disease known as severe porphyria. This is a genetic disease. One symptom is a severe reaction to light, exposure to which produces skin lesions. These lesions may ulcerate, resulting in the destruction of cartilage or bone. The tissue destruction frequently occurs in the nose, ears and fingers. A brownish pigmentation of the facial skin may take place. The victim may become deranged, falling victim to mild hysteria, manic-depressive psychosis or delirium. Hair may grow on the face.

These are all werewolf-like features but this rare disease probably accounts for few cases of werewolfery. In its most severe form this disease is extremely rare – too rare to help us explain something so widespread as the werewolf phenomenon.

Perhaps the only conclusion we can safely draw is that no single explanation accounts for all reports of werewolfery. Among the possible explanations, one or more of which may apply in any given case, for individuals' belief that they can turn into wolves are: psychosis, hallucinogenic drug effects, religious mania, mistaken observation, coincidence, manifestations of archetypal behavior, hoax, delusional behavior brought on by fear of possession, immersion in folkloric beliefs – or perhaps, just perhaps, a bite from a werewolf!

Gordon Stein (1941-96): Author and activist for atheism and religious skepticism.

FATE January 1988

WOULD YOU BELIEVE A WEREWOLF?
Douglas Hill and Pat Williams

Werewolf stories abound in the folklore of practically every country in the world. Germany has its *werewolf,* Spain its *lob ombre,* Portugal its *lob omem,* Italy its *lupo manaro,* and France and French-speaking nations have more than their share of *loups-garous.* Furthermore, the werewolf has its cousins in countries where wolves never have been: India has tales of were-tigers, Africa of were-hyenas. Even in places where there are or once were plenty of wolves, such as Russia and France, tales exist of were-dogs, bears, cats, foxes – even toads.

The depth of terror the werewolf can inspire and its hold on men's imaginations pervade the world's folklore, and two real factors underlie the fear. First, wolves (the animals themselves) have been deadly enemies of men almost since each first evolved – perhaps the deadliest enemy, at least in the northern hemisphere, where they have been hunted relentlessly in an attempt to exterminate them. (Other dangerous animals are hunted to be controlled; it seems where wolves are concerned men grow hysterical and seek to wipe them out completely.) Extermination has succeeded in many places. There are no longer any wolves in Germany, Switzerland, Britain or the United States (except Alaska). It was thought that France (which suffered more than any country from wolves in the past) was also free of them; but a small pack was seen there in 1963 and made headlines internationally, a reflection of the widespread fearful fascination of the animals. Recently wolves have been seen in Northern Italy and in Canada (where a man was attacked in northern Ontario in 1963) as well as in Spain, Portugal, Poland and Turkey.

But wolves are not only (in general) ferocious predators who hunt in packs and who don't mind what kind of meat they eat; they also have a certain eeriness about them which readily prompts a link with the supernatural. They are semi-nocturnal, silent, greyish in color; their catlike eyes glow red in reflected firelight, yellow-green in moonlight; and their chilling banshee-like howl completes the picture of a not-quite-natural beast. They are animals, in other words, with something demonic about them. From there it is a short easy step to linking them with the devil's legions and with witchcraft.

To the 16th- and 17th-century experts, if a werewolf was much the same as a witch then one became a werewolf the way one became a witch – through a pact with the devil. Once the pact was concluded, the devil conferred upon the initiate the power of magical metamorphosis. Now this power was just one of the talents acquired by a new witch. But in a great many tales and demonologists' accounts, it seems that a large percentage of werewolves were only werewolves; they lacked the witches' other powers – of sorcery or of flight, for instance. It seems as if most werewolves had petitioned the devil *only* for the lycanthropic ability.

Also, the folklore of most nations offers many methods of becoming a werewolf other than by entering into a contract with the devil. Some of these semi-magical procedures did not directly involve any diabolism. In Italian folk belief, anyone conceived at the time of the new moon would become a werewolf; and so would anyone who slept overnight in the open on a Friday under a full moon. In the Balkan Peninsula – fertile ground for werewolf and vampire legends – a certain nameless flower would turn anyone who ate it into a werewolf. Drinking water from a real wolf's footprint, drinking from a stream where a wolf pack drank or eating a wolf's brains – these are some of the ways according to folklore of becoming a werewolf, intentionally or not.

In many legends, metamorphosis into a werewolf can be accomplished only by some complicated ceremony – in which the man must strip, smear on the ointment, say an incantation, and (always important) put on the wolf-skin belt or sometimes even an entire wolf hide. But often the process is simplified. Some folktales tell of men changing into werewolves merely by stripping under the full moon and rolling around in the dirt for a few moments. In others, a man achieves the metamorphosis by removing his clothes under a full moon and urinating in a circle drawn on the ground. In still others, all that is needed is to remove human clothing and put on a wolf's skin – or just the belt. As for changing back, a few authorities say that parts of the ritual need to be reversed. Others say the wolf-to-human transformation happens automatically when the night is over.

During the night itself a werewolf's activities are generally limited to the very wolfish practices of hunting, killing and eating. (This is aside from those demonic wolves who spent their time at sabbats.) Some tales of werewolves have them limiting their ravaging to flocks and herds in the countryside; but most often lycanthropy means cannibalism; the werewolf hungers for human flesh. Though werewolves were seldom particular, they were generally thought to prefer the flesh of children (remember that witches were often accused of eating children at sabbats) and especially of young girls. A self-confessed werewolf in 17th-century France, an imbecilic boy named Grenier, boasted that he had killed and eaten many young girls and was promptly tried and imprisoned by the authorities who took him at his word. This link between lycanthropy and another tortuous word, *parthenophagy*, (a delight in the flesh of girls), recurs again and again; and since the parthenophagous werewolf was usually a child rapist as well, here we have links between the werewolf myth and two age-old and almost universal human taboos; cannibalism and sexual perversion.

Both figure strongly in a famous case of werewolfery in 16th-century Germany – the case of Peter Stubb, or Stump. It is one of the most detailed (and therefore, for us, most valuable) accounts of a supposed werewolf's activities ever written.

The attacks, capture, trial, torture and execution of the werewolf Peter Stubb.

Stubb achieved werefwolfhood by a pact with the devil. His purpose (according to an English pamphlet on him published in 1590) was to exercise "his malice on men, women and children, in the shape of some beast, whereby he might live without dread of danger of life and unknown to be the executor of any bloody enterprise which he meant to commit." The devil gave him a wolf-skin belt; Stubb merely needed to put it on in order to metamorphose. Then he began 25 years of terrorizing the countryside.

He killed and ate cattle and sheep occasionally; he killed many people who had at one time offended him (but seldom ate them if they were adult and male); and especially he raped, killed and ate women and girls. The pamphlet says: "...he would walk up and down and if he could spy either maid, wife or child that his eyes liked and his heart lusted after, he would wait their issuing out of the city or town, if he could by any means get them alone, he would in the fields ravish them, and after in his wolfish likeness cruelly murder them...". Thus, within a few years, "he had murdered 13 young children and two goodly young women big with child."

The pamphlet goes on describing his evil. Stubb committed incest with his daughter (who had a child by him) and his sister, and had many other "concubines" – including, for seven years, a succubus sent by the devil. Among all his murders during the years he was a werewolf, one was by far the worst: the pamphlet tells us he killed and ate his own son.

Finally, the populace's attempts to catch and kill the terrible wolf succeeded. Pursued in his wolf form by men and many dogs, Stubb tried to shake off the pursuers by removing the belt and changing back into a man. But the pursuers, realizing what must have happened, "had him incontinent before the magistrates to be examined." Though the belt was never found, there was enough evidence: the fact that Stubb had suddenly appeared before the pursuers' eyes, the fact of his incest and other sins. He was found guilty, tortured horribly, and executed – and his head was mounted on a pole outside the town of Bedburg as a warning and a trophy.

Like most of the devil's human servants, Stubb seems to have given his captors no trouble once he was caught; he was executed the way anyone, supernatural power or no, would have been executed if they had committed a capital crime. The way also that witches were executed (few witches were ever said to have escaped the Inquisition by exercising their magical powers). The experts said that the devil left his servants to their own devices once they were caught (that is, once their usefulness was at an end), and simply waited for their souls to arrive in hell. So no special means were necessary to put an end to werewolves. They merely had to be caught, the way ordinary wolves and ordinary heretics were caught.

Even where folklore did not relate werewolves to the devil, plain means were often sufficient to destroy them – means that would be employed against real wolves. They were killed according to various accounts with knives and clubs and guns. And usually when wounded or dead the wolves automatically reverted to human form. There is a 16th-century French tale of a hunter who beat off an attack by a fierce wolf, and in the fight cut off one of the beast's paws. He put the paw in his pouch and set off home; on the way he met a friend, told the story of the battle, and reached for the paw to show it. But he found in his pouch a woman's hand, wearing a gold ring. The hunter thought he recognized the hand, and rushed home to find – as he suspected – his wife bandaging the bleeding stump of her arm. The wife was shortly tried by the local authorities and burned.

Where the werewolf is thought to be demonically possessed, exorcism is the usual cure. But there are many nonreligious, quasi-magical procedures that people can use to rid themselves of werewolves when normal means fail.

If the werewolf cannot be killed or cured, a variety of materials will at least keep him away. Rye, mistletoe, ash and yew trees have been considered good protection in Britain. Some authorities say that werewolves fear running water (perhaps relating lycanthropy to hydrophobia, seeing a werewolf in a real wolf gone rabid). And there are also ways of knowing that a man is a werewolf and thus protecting oneself by keeping away from him. Such signs include straight, slanting eyebrows meeting over the nose; long, curved, reddish fingernails; small ears set low on the head; an exceptionally long third finger on each hand; and sometimes merely extreme hairiness, especially on the hands and feet. There are no generally accepted ways of distinguishing a werewolf in his wolf shape from an ordinary wolf, except that the werewolf is said (rather vaguely) to be bigger, fiercer and hungrier. But in some folktales the werewolf is a human with a wolf's head or a wolf with human hands.

In one case related by Claude Seignolle, supposed to have occurred about the turn of the century, a French farmer saw two wolves and climbed a tree to avoid them. They hadn't seen him, however, and so he was able to watch and listen – and to recognize them easily as werewolves. Not only did they converse in human voices; but one took a snuffbox from under his tail and offered it to the other. They dropped the box, and the farmer later recovered it and traced its owner – a local man. The farmer (who died in 1927) told the story often, but never revealed the names – until one of the two alleged werewolves died an apparently natural death some years later and it was found that every morning his gravestone showed fresh scratches apparently made by the paws of a wolf.

The modern British writer Robert Eisler has produced a far-reaching anthropological theory concerning sadism, masochism and lycanthropy based on his knowledge of ancient history and legend. To simplify greatly Eisler's ideas: first, he amasses evidence to show that man was not always carnivorous or aggressive; that like most primates and many primitives today, ancient men were vegetarian and frugivorous, given neither to war nor to violence nor to sexual violence especially. But this idyllic state was altered by changing circumstances such as the coming of an ice age. To survive primeval man had to find new food, so he turned to meat; he had to cover his nudity, so he made fur clothing. He learned to hunt and to do so in packs for better results. And the upheaval that this gradual transformation caused left its scars on man's collective unconscious (Eisler borrows the term from Jung) and produced sado-masochism, its related guilt feelings – and the werewolf myth.

Eisler's theory offers attractive explanations for many aspects of werewolfery. For instance, the sexual emphasis: primeval man in his wolf pack had the choice between fighting the pack leader in order to get a woman or stealing a woman from a more peaceful tribe. Hence, later werewolves are seen as rapists. And as for cannibalism, presumably the ancient fur-clad tribes ate whatever they could find when the glaciers ruined the north land and the human packs moved south, where people might still be frugivorous and peaceful. The same way that much later the berserkers moved south to pillage; and that the wolves themselves would move during a hard winter. And if you were an inhabitant of a southern community and had your village robbed and burned and your women stolen and raped by fur-clad, howling berserkers one day and the next day ravaged by a pack of four-legged wolves, would you not tend to see little difference between man and wolf? And assume that they could change their shape at will?

This leaves us only one more factor that may have contributed to werewolf tales: the pathological condition that also is called lycanthropy. A sufferer will be fully convinced that he is a wild animal; he will howl, desire raw meat, perhaps even run on all fours. It is possible that many specific werewolf stories have grown out of cases of actual lycanthropy – which according to Rossell Hope Robbins were fairly prevalent in the 16th and 17th centuries. (The mentally defective Jean Grenier, mentioned before, may have been this kind of lycanthrope; the disease is often linked with defectiveness.) The disease gives the sufferer the hallucination that he has actually metamorphosed or at least that his teeth and claws have lengthened. Some lycanthropes (in 17th-century accounts) assured people that they were actually wolves but that their hair grew on the inside. It is also possible, remembering the drugs employed by witches, that the ointment used in the metamorphosis spells, plus autosuggestions, may have induced hallucination in would-be werewolves who did not suffer from the disease lycanthropy.

To sum up then: adding together all the possibilities – unconscious archetypal fears and memories, garbled and exaggerated history transmitted orally, mental disease, hallucinatory drugs, and man's age-old fear and hatred of the wolf – it is no wonder that the werewolf legend grew up, spread so widely and persists today. And it does persist. In Bourg-la-Reine, France, in 1930 a farmer had a reputation as a sorcerer (his house was found to contain all the paraphernalia, including amulets and wax dolls) and was firmly believed by his neighbors to take the shape of a wolf at night. In 1946 in America a trading post on a Navajo Indian reservation was terrorized by rumors of an Indian werewolf who raided flocks, dug up and robbed graves and killed and ate women.

According to the late American psychoanalyst Dr. Nandor Fodor, "The old savage lycanthropic beliefs have been relegated to our dream life where they are still active conditions and are exploited for the representation of criminal motives, while the transformation is used symbolically as self-denunciation for secret deeds, fantasies or desires." Some of the dreams Fodor recounts to prove this lend weight to Eisler's idea that those scars on the collective unconscious are by no means healed.

Excerpted from The Supernatural *by Douglas Hill and Pat Williams. Copyright 1965 by Aldus Books, Ltd. Published by Hawthorn Books, Inc., 70 Fifth Ave., New York, NY.*

FATE September 1969

THE MASK OF THE WEREWOLF
Hugh H. Trotti, Jr.

The ancient Romans left us a legacy of, among other things, two masks: that of Comedy and that of Tragedy. In 1987 a paper was published which led me to wonder if they had left yet a third mask to history – one which was to enter the medieval world in the form of bizarre tales of adventure, and descend to us in the form of Hollywood's own style of entertainment. The mask in question is one which seems to show the face of a wolf.

A wolf's mask would not be particularly puzzling if it were not placed on the face of a statue of a man. The obvious result seems to be the emergence of the "werewolf," known in French as the *loup-garou*. If the creature in question is not to be viewed as a product of imagination, then what caused the belief?

There may well be a solution to the "mystery" of folk belief in the werewolf. And such a solution may point to something very simple and even obvious.

First, let's look at the shamanism of the prehistoric world. We know of the Amerind "medicine man" and various Siberian shamanistic beliefs of a somewhat similar nature. Indeed, as Davenport and Jochim contended in the September 1988 issue of the periodical *Antiquity*, such beliefs may reach far back in time-perhaps even in excess of 12,000 years. The caverns of France contain more than one figure that seems to portray the shaman-type figure: men wearing the masks of various animals (although the interpretation of such figures must always be somewhat in doubt). We know of the so-called "Sorcerer" figure from the famous Trois Freres cave, and there are others.

Early humans may well have identified with animals, and the contention in Davenport and Jochim's article that the "falling" figure in the scene in the Lascaux cave represents a shaman type entering a mystic state by "becoming" a bird through trance (or at least enhancing his powers through the aid of a bird "spirit helper") seems a plausible contention. In a sense, the shaman may be in the process of becoming a "were-bird." His figure, drawn in front of a wounded bison and near a "bird" symbol on a wand or stick, may indeed represent a man "in tune" with nature by virtue of the aid of his animal "spirit helper."

This sounds like witchcraft beliefs concerning "familiars" such as cats or other animals. I find it surprising that a belief could exist for so many thousands of years in such a similar form. Nonetheless, shamanism of a type did exist among the Scythians in the first millennium BCE. Michael Grant has noted in the *Rise of the Greeks* the spread of Scythian shamanistic ideas into Greece via a Thracian route, and, of course, we know of the Greek trade with the north shore of the Black Sea during those times. What affected the Greeks would affect the Romans in later eras. And, myths aside, there is the story of a werewolf in Petronius Arbiter's *Satyricon*.

During the age of the Viking explorations, the Vikings seem to have occasionally had a habit of working themselves up into animal-like conduct. Becoming "berserk" in order to gain increased strength or fearsomeness, such warriors might be thought to be bear-like or wolf-like in their rages. Could the werewolf be linked to such historical behavior?

A new possibility

A new and simple origin for European belief in the werewolf may point back through Rome to Egypt. This is suggested by the publication of Arelene Wolinski's paper "Egyptian Masks: The Priest and His Role" in the American periodical *Archaeology* of January/February 1987. Though the article has no mention of werewolves, it is the basis of a new possibility of understanding and explaining the existence of the werewolf concept in a very clear and simple way.

In Wolinski's view, when we see Egyptian paintings of animal-headed human-like figures, sometimes the intention is to depict an officiating priest and not a god. The key to knowing that we are viewing a man in a mask is, according to Wolinski, to note the two dangling items having the appearance of broad ribbons that hang from the mask onto the front of the chest of masked figures. Called *lappets*, they may have been weighted to make the mask sit more securely. At any rate, they indicate the priest in mask. Again according to Wolinski, the priest wearing his mask would have joined in various processions and other ceremonies of a sometimes public nature.

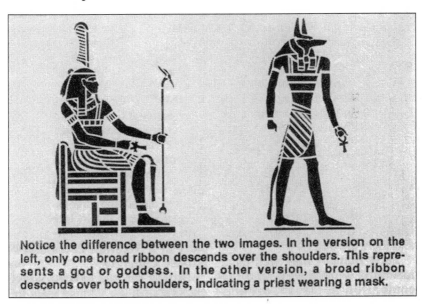

Notice the difference between the two images. In the version on the left, only one broad ribbon descends over the shoulders. This represents a god or goddess. In the other version, a broad ribbon descends over both shoulders, indicating a priest wearing a mask.

Clearly, a priest wearing the wolf-like jackal-headed mask of the god Anubis might be easily misunderstood by foreigners in Egypt. Is the Anubis priest, walking along in a religious procession, the original werewolf? (Wolinski makes no such claim, of course, though the Anubis figure is the one chiefly used to portray the basic idea of priestly masking in the article.) Remembering the history of the Greeks and Romans in Egypt, it is certain that (Wolinski's contention being correct) many Europeans would have viewed the Anubis priest with his jackal head during the long centuries of polytheism. Possibilities of gossip and misunderstanding are obvious.

The Anubis cult even made its way to Rome. Wolinski illustrates a Roman statue of a figure titled "Hermanubis" (a statue of a man in a Roman tunic with a dog's head). The Christian author Cyprian scoffed at former senators lowering their dignity by going about with dog's masks on their heads, and Juvenal, the Roman playwright, thought it unpriestly for a priest to wear such a mask.

From this evidence, it seems clear that there were priests of the Hermanubis cult wandering about in Rome itself, as well as Hermanubis statues. The very name "Hermanubis" comes from a joining of the Greco-Roman god Mercury, also known as Hermes, with the Egyptian Anubis. The Romans who took part in public ceremonies as priests of the god would be seen by people throughout their empire.

Germanic peoples were recruited into the Roman armies as some of Rome's chief defenders toward the end of empire. At that time, Rome no longer took part in her own defense. Even so, the Germanic peoples overthrew the Western Roman Empire. We know that the werewolf shape-changing idea is found in Germanic legend and that the Franks, themselves Germanic in origin, possessed werewolf tales in the medieval period. The connection, then, from Egypt to Rome, and then to other parts of Europe, seems fairly obvious.

Where were the hippopotamus-men?

You may wonder why there are no "hippopotamus-men" or "lion-men" in northern European legends. Well, there were no lions or hippos in Europe in the medieval period. There were wolves, however, and they had a strong resemblance to the jackal face of Anubis.

During the Dark Ages, sophisticated knowledge of the nature of ancient cults would be lost. The Church had no interest in the perpetuation of such knowledge. A garbled tradition of the existence of a man-wolf might be the result of the passage of time.

If Wolinski's hypothesis is correct (and she does cite other, earlier authorities for the masking hypothesis, going back to Maspero), we have a very simple origin for the idea of the werewolf in Europe. We have no need to bring forward an attempted connection to palaeolithic shamanism, Scythian shamanism, various human diseases, or Viking berserk behavior. Some of these things may have colored the concept in later years, but with Wolinski's evidence we have a more simple and direct origin for a concept which is seen to be a real and tangible historical phenomenon of known nature.

No one would say that Marco Polo's huge striped lions were imaginary: we simply know that he must have seen tigers. Again, many scholars have pointed out the somewhat more tenuous idea that the "unicorn" was simply the Indian rhinoceros which Alexander the Great had found. After all, if a hippo can be a horse (hippopotamus from the Greek for "river-horse"), then why not a rhino? The idea presented here is that the werewolf concept may fall into the group, however limited such a group may be, of bizarre beliefs that have fairly simple beginnings.

The "periodical" elements involved in the belief (i.e., the connection to the full moon or to certain times of the month in the old French tales) may be suggestive of religious origins in the sense of periodic ceremonies.

The Roman statue pictured in the article by Wolinski is a more direct source of information than random references in such ancient sources as Herodotus (e.g. Persian Wars, where the *Neuri* – a Scythian tribe – were said to become wolves once a year). If the ancient Europeans after the fall of the Western Roman Empire were largely illiterate, viewing statues with the heads of "wolves" and seeing men walking in rituals (at least in Rome) wearing wolf (actually jackal) masks would have impressed the Germanic recruits and entered their sagas and tales. Fine distinctions between wolves, dogs, and jackals likely would be lost over the ages as the folktales, with their stories of werewolves, spread over Europe.

FATE February 1990

MAN, MYTH, OR MONSTER?
Joe P. Giannone

During the summer of 1764, in the region of France known as Lozere, a series of brutal killings began. Swiftly and mercilessly, young children were torn apart as they played in the fields near their homes. In each case, the victim was found with his head ripped from his body; his flesh horribly pulled from his bones. The local villagers delayed only a short time before beginning their hunt for the evil creature that had brought death upon their quaint hamlets. It was clear to all who had seen the mutilated bodies that the victims had fallen prey to a werewolf.

The werewolf has existed in popular legend since Biblical times, although the actual term "werewolf" wasn't used until the Middle Ages when an early set of Anglo-Saxon rules of government, the laws of Canute, labeled a violent outlaw as a "verevolf." Even though the popular terminology did not exist at the time, the mythical founders of Rome, Romulus and Remus, were said to have been raised by a she-wolf, a rearing that instilled within them many "wolf-like" attributes. The stories have continued throughout history, into modern times, with the werewolf taking on an ever more violent and malicious cast.

What is a werewolf?

By strict definition, a werewolf is a lycanthrope, a human that can change his form, through one means or another, from that of a man to that of a wolf. The term lycanthrope is not limited only to werewolves, but applies also to men (and women) capable of changing themselves into a vast array of animals, including baboons, cats and gazelles. The werewolf, however, appears to be the most common form of lycanthropy attested to in legend and historic eyewitness accounts.

The Beast of Gevaudan

The case already mentioned, that of the beast that terrorized France in the 18th century, is perhaps one of the most convincing – and frightening – cases of the werewolf phenomenon to be documented to date. The mysterious creature, known to history as the Beast of Gevaudan, convinced an entire region of France that werewolves do, indeed, exist.

The first sighting of the Beast of Gevaudan occurred on a warm June day, as a shepherd girl dutifully stood watch over a herd of cattle. The girl heard a sound, turned to investigate, and saw before her an unusually large wolf, with strangely colored hair of a reddish tint. The creature lunged for the girl, ripping her flesh, but before the animal could regroup for a second attack, the girl's oxen had charged and attacked the beast, frightening it back into the thick woods from which it came.

The episode was regarded merely as an attack by an unusually brazen wolf, more than likely half-crazed with hunger. It would soon become obvious to all concerned that the beast's motivation could not be explained away in such a simple manner.

Soon after the first attack, the creature struck again, this time killing a 15-year-old girl near a village called Habats. Slightly more than a month later, three more children, a girl and two boys, were killed, mutilated and partially eaten.

The victims were all attacked in a similar fashion, with the wolf-like creature lunging directly at their chests, knocking them to the ground, and quickly ripping their faces from their skulls with its razor-sharp fangs. By November of 1764, 10 people had died in a similar fashion.

The wolf shot by François Antoine displayed at the court of Louis XV.

An overwhelming fear gripped the people of the surrounding countryside – understandably so, considering the fact that their small population was being swiftly killed off and they were powerless to stop the creature responsible.

Send in the soldiers

Eventually, the news of the attacks reached the French government, and a unit of dragoons stationed at the town of Clermont-Ferrand were ordered to hunt down and kill the beast.

The dragoons, under the command of a Captain Jean Duhamel, scoffed at the idea that their aid was to be enlisted in order to hunt down a wolf, but proceeded to the Gevaudan region as instructed.

In the month that followed, the group of confident soldiers found and killed over 100 wolves. Sure that the problem had been taken care of, the men left the area, still surprised that they should have been asked to accomplish such a mundane task. But the soldiers were quickly proven overconfident and foolhardy.

As soon as the dragoons had left the area, the attacks from the beast resumed, this time with the murder of a seven-year-old boy. Before the end of the year, two more young girls were killed.

The townspeople were now gripped by a fear deeper than any they had previously known. What was this creature that was systematically killing off their young? How could the dragoons have killed over 100 wolves, and missed the one animal responsible for the killings? To many of the villagers, the answer was obvious – the killer was a werewolf.

Curious indications

Many puzzling aspects of this case seem to indicate that the creature was indeed more than just a bloodthirsty wolf. Many traps were set for the creature, and many animals were caught within the traps, but somehow the murderous Beast of Gevaudan always managed to avoid capture. The creature had ample natural prey, but in many instances witnesses observed the animal attack a human victim while ignoring livestock, such as lambs and goats, that were left frolicking in a nearby field. Why had the creature decided to adopt an exclusive diet of humans? All of these questions were answered by the local villagers with cries of "werewolf!"

The murderer found?

Other soldiers were dispatched, including famous wolf hunters of the day. Organized hunts for the animal became a common occurrence, but the horrible attacks continued with the beast always managing to slyly avoid its pursuers. It was not until two years after the first attack that a wolf was shot and the brutal killing spree came to an end.

On one of the regular wolf hunts, a middle-aged villager by the name of Jean Chastel was walking casually through a portion of the forest known as la Sogne-d'Auvert. Two years of hunts had failed to produce the beast, and most of the common wolves of the area had been killed in previous searches, so Mr. Chastel was understandably surprised when he was confronted by a huge, snarling beast, complete with the unusual coat of red hair described by witnesses of the creature's violent attacks. Chastel quickly aimed his gun and fired. The animal fell to the ground, kicked violently and finally died.

Not an ordinary wolf

At a nearby town, it was concluded after a crude autopsy that the fallen creature was, without question, the Beast of Gevaudan. When the stomach of the animal was opened, the local coroners found the shoulder bone belonging to a girl that had been killed only one day earlier.

The examiners had also concluded that the animal was not an ordinary wolf, and the creature's corpse was packaged and sent to more experienced authorities for further examination. Unfortunately, before the carcass had reached its destination, it had rotted to such an advanced state of decomposition that it was impossible to conduct a thorough examination.

In the two years since its first attack, the Beast of Gevaudan had killed and mutilated over 60 people. The creature had succeeded in eluding hundreds of hunters, and thousands of traps. Could an individual honestly be blamed for believing that the beast was somehow graced with supernatural powers? The great majority of the inhabitants of the Gevaudan region of France had no doubt in their minds that the creature which was finally killed was no less than the manifestation of evil known as the werewolf.

Modern occurrences

Occurrences of apparent lycanthropy have been just as common in modern times. Frequent reports by well-respected psychiatrists of individuals exhibiting lycanthropic mental aberrations are evidence of this.

Such a case was reported in the October 1977 issue of the *American Journal of Psychiatry.* The case report states that a 49-year-old woman was admitted on an urgent basis for psychiatric observation because she was "feeling like an animal with claws." The woman told examining doctors that she felt as if she were no longer in control of her body, and she often declared, "a voice is coming out of me." Her husband supported her claims by reporting that throughout their 20-year marriage she had been prone to bestiality, delusions of changing into a wolf, and nightmares of prowling the neighborhood as an animal. A week before the patient was admitted to the hospital for treatment, she had been overcome by an attack of her "lycanthropic" urges. At a family gathering she stripped naked, fell to the floor on all fours and adopted the behavior of a wolf. After recovering, the woman insisted that "the devil had come into her body, and she had become an animal."

The doctors, examining the patient, began to pursue a course of treatment that included group counseling and neuroleptic medication. The treatments slowly began to reverse the woman's attacks, but during the first three weeks of her treatment, she would fall into trance-like states, and say things like, "I am a wolf of the night, I am a wolf woman of the day ... I have claws, teeth, fangs, hair, and anguish is my prey at night. I am what I am, and will always roam the earth long after death." The patient also claimed to be frightened when looking at herself in the mirror, as she was confronted with a vision of a wolf that was "dark, deep, evil, and full of revenge."

After nine weeks of treatment, the patient had stabilized and was released with the advice that she should continue to take the medication that seemed to lessen her lycanthropic attacks. When her treatment was terminated, the woman remarked, "I don't intend to give up my search for what I lack ... my search for such a hairy creature. I will haunt the graveyards for a tall, dark man that I intend to find."

The final report by the patient's doctors included this statement: "Lycanthropy is a rare phenomenon but it does exist. It should be regarded as a symptom complex and not a diagnostic entity. Furthermore, although it may generally be an expression of an underlying schizophrenic condition, at least five other diagnostic entities must be considered."

Causes of lycanthropy
The doctors then describe, in depth, these five "entities" or causes for lycanthropy, among them schizophrenia, hysterical neurosis, and organic brain syndrome. Satisfied by their findings, the doctors sent the curious report to the *American Journal of Psychiatry*.

Questions remain
While it might make interesting reading to other medical professionals, the report falls far short of being a true explanation of lycanthropy. Schizophrenia is a relatively well understood disease of the mind (at least the basic treatment is well understood) but why should the disease choose to manifest itself in the form of lycanthropy? Why would such an obsession be so common throughout history? And how can schizophrenia explain an instance such as that witnessed by the victims of the Beast of Gevaudan, in which a creature seems to appear in the "fully transformed" guise of a wolf. Organic brain syndrome (a chemical problem within the brain) may explain a mental transformation, but how could a delusion be responsible for an actual physical transformation?

The Werewolf of Antoine De Pizon

Others have offered alternative explanations, such as that propounded by Jean Grenier, the werewolf of Antoine de Pizon. Grenier was born the son of a poor laborer in the small village of South Antoine de Pizon. It appears that 19th-century France offered the boy little of interest, and he spent many hours wandering the local woods alone.

When a series of wolf attacks began in the area, young Jean was only too glad to confess to the crimes, claiming that he would change into the guise of a wolf before attacking his victims. When the boy was brought before the local court for questioning, he displayed an uncanny knowledge of the attacks, reciting a list of attacks, times that they occurred, and accurate descriptions of the victims. When a young girl, a survivor of one of the attacks, was brought to court to testify, she confirmed detailed statements already made by Jean Grenier, but claimed that Jean was not the attacker. Instead, the young girl insisted that she had been set upon by "an animal resembling a wolf, but as being shorter and stouter, its hair was red, its tail stumpy, and its head smaller than that of a genuine wolf."

It is interesting to note here that both the creature sighted by the young girl and the Beast of Gevaudan were said to have red hair, certainly strong support for the idea that this "animal" is a consistent and genuine manifestation. Eventually, Jean Grenier's father was called to testify, and summarily confirmed his son's testimony, informing the court that his son had even gone so far as to tell him the story of how he had become a werewolf. Young Jean was again brought before the court, and when asked to relate the story of how he became a lycanthrope, he told the following tale:

How to become a werewolf

"When I was ten or eleven years old, my neighbor, Duthillaire, introduced me, in the depths of the forest, to a M. de la Forest, a black man who signed me with his nail, and then gave to me and Duthillaire a salve and a wolf-skin. From that time, I have run about the country as a wolf."

The boy continued to relate details of the local attacks that could have been known only to the murderer, and eventually the judge hearing the case was left no alternative but to find the boy guilty.

Placing aside the decision of whether or not the boy was a lycanthrope, the judge declared Jean mentally and morally impaired and sentenced him to life imprisonment within the walls of a monastery at Bordeaux. When admitted to the monastery, the boy fell to all fours, and frantically ran around the grounds. Discovering a heap of raw and bloody meat scraps thrown out by the order's cook, young Jean "fell upon it and devoured it in an incredibly short space of time."

The boy's behavior eventually demanded full imprisonment. Seven years after his arrival at the religious establishment, he was described as "diminutive in stature, very shy, and unwilling to look anyone in the face. His eyes were deep set and restless; his teeth long and protruding; his nails black, and in places worn away; his mind was completely barren; he seemed unable to comprehend the smallest things."

Was he or wasn't he?

Jean Grenier, alone in his cell, died at the age of 20, leaving behind a stream of unanswered questions:

Was Jean a lycanthrope? It was certainly established that he had committed the murders. But did he kill as a wolf or simply as a demented victim of some mental disease?

Modern men of medicine would assure us that Jean, as well as all other cases of lycanthropy, could be explained with a diagnosis of various mental impairments. The observers of werewolf attacks throughout history would surely disagree.

They would unquestionably testify that they had been witness to a vision of evil somehow more, and somehow less, than human.

Bibliography

Otten, Charlotte R. A *Lycanthropy Reader-Werewolves in Western Culture* (Syracuse University Press New York, 1986.)

Rowland, Beryl. *Animals with Human Faces* (University of Tennessee Press, Knoxville, 1973.)

Copper, Basil. *The Werewolf in Legend, Fact and Art* (St. Martin's Press, New York, 1977.)

FATE April 1992

WHO OR WHAT WAS THE BEAST OF LE GEVAUDAN?

Andrew E. Rothovius

Along the edge of the Auvergne Plateau in south-central France lies an 80-mile stretch of rugged, mountainous country known as Le Gevaudan. Despite the relative nearness of such populous cities as Lyons and Toulouse, this area remains to a large extent isolated and primitive. Its hardy peasantry, struggling for generation after generation to wrest a living from the barren moors and ridges, is reputed as fearless and resolute a race as any in Europe.

Yet, there was an occasion two centuries ago when these brave folk were driven to despair by the depredations of a monstrous creature whose true nature is still a mystery. Known to historians as the "Beast of Le Gevaudan," it is usually described as an enormous wolf. It is quite true that wolves survived in the mountains of Le Gevaudan longer than anywhere in France; they were hunted there much later than the time of the Beast. However, the facts of the case, as given in the official records, cannot be satisfactorily accounted for on this supposition.

In almost every instance the Beast tore out the heart of its victims and drank their blood, leaving the bodies otherwise untouched. It walked on its hind legs like a bear and peered in demoniac fashion through the windows of the homes its attacks had bereaved. These are not the normal actions of a wolf.

The Beast first made himself known in mid-July 1764, when a little girl, of the village of St. Etienne de Lugdares, who had strayed from her task as shepherdess, was found dead with her heart torn out of her body.

Within a few days five more children from nearby villages suffered similar fates. As news of these killings spread, panic flamed across Le Gevaudan. The alarmed peasants hurried to bring their sheep and cattle down from the mountain pastures and with them the children who customarily tended them in the summer.

No one as yet had seen the creature responsible for the ghastly murders, though many whispered the dread name *loup-garou* – werewolf.

A few weeks passed without further attacks and the district was beginning to quiet down. Then late in August a peasant woman at Langogne reported she had seen an animal of terrifying appearance. It had frightened away her dogs which were used to fighting wolves; but her cattle had faced the monster with lowered horns and it had then run off into the woods. Her description was so fantastic that she was laughed at and accused of imagining the incident.

However, within a week or two the child murders recommenced – the mysterious creature apparently having waited until the peasants got over their first alarm and again permitted their children to go unattended into the lonely pastures. Five more youngsters were found slain and mutilated in the same way as the earlier victims had been mutilated.

Soon thereafter at the village of Zulianges a brave peasant named Jean-Pierre Pourcher, well known for his courage, saw from his barn door one evening a strange creature walking down the road. Immediately guessing it to be the killer of the children, he seized his musket and fired at it. In the gathering dusk his aim was poor and the monster fled, apparently unhurt.

The description he gave of it tallied closely with the report by the Langogne woman. It had walked upright like a man and seemed to have something like horseshoes on its hind feet. As big as a large donkey, it

The Beast of Gevaudan.

had reddish hair, a snout resembling a pig's, an open mouth, short ears and long tail with white tip.

Pourcher further stated, in his report to the authorities, that before he fired at it, the monster had made various peculiar gestures with its front feet.

Murder now became an almost daily occurrence. The Beast began to attack groups of several persons. The survivors invariably agreed in describing their assailant as similar to the creature seen by Pourcher. At the village of Chanaleilles it seized a child named Jean Panafieux. Several older lads, headed by one named Andre Portefaix, attempted to rescue Jean. They attacked the monster with pitchforks and knives tied to long sticks; but after a desperate struggle, in which one other child was slain and half of Jean's head was bitten away by the monster's teeth, it managed to escape.

An appeal for help now was sent by the terrified peasantry to the Royal Court at Versailles. Louis XV, bored and restless during the interval between his two famous mistresses, Mesdames Pompadour and Du Barry, was receptive to the sensational news from Le Gevaudan. He gave the brave Portefaix youth a commission and pension in the artillery and dispatched a company of dragoons, or light cavalry, under Captain Duhamel to hunt down the Beast.

Before the troops could arrive, the monster attacked and murdered a 14-year-old boy, Jean Chateauneuf, on January 15, 1765. As the boy's father sat mourning his child in his darkened home on the following evening, the Beast placed its forepaws on the window sill and glared in at him with a demoniac expression. The father shouted for help but in the deepening winter dusk the creature easily made off, mocking with antic gestures its frightened and half-hearted pursuers.

Dubamel's dragoons reached Le Gevaudan early in February. They picked up the Beast's tracks in the snow on the 6th. The next day they located it in a thicket and fired five shots at it. Giving a loud howl, it sprang up and ran into a dense underbrush where the soldiers, believing they had inflicted mortal wounds, did not choose to follow it. Close by, however, they found the mutilated body of a 14-year-old girl who had been missing for some time.

The murders now ceased and Captain Duhamel concluded that the Beast had been slain. He departed with his troops. Hardly had they left, however, than another child was found killed and mutilated on March 4. As the snows melted and the cattle again were led up into the mountain pastures, a renewed slaughter of child shepherds followed.

Scarcely a day passed, in that terrible summer of 1765, without a child falling victim to the monster, now apparently fully recovered from its wounds. There is not a parish in the entire Le Gevaudan district, whose registers do not contain a long and dreadful list of children slain by the Beast in that nightmare year. Bands of armed peasants scoured the mountains, killing more than 100 wolves, but they never caught up with the murdering monster.

New appeals for assistance were directed to Versailles but, having discovered Du Barry, Louis XV had lost interest in the mass tragedy in the remote province. Not until early in 1766, in response to urgent representations from his privy councilors, did he finally dispatch a second expedition, this time headed by his personal gunbearer, Antoine.

Instead of proceeding directly to Le Gevaudan, however, Antoine headed into the mountains of Central Auvergne where a great wolf had been reported. He tracked it down, shot it, and exhibited the pelt as belonging to the Beast of Le Gevaudan. Then he returned to Versailles, where the Court proclaimed the emergency at an end.

Unfortunately for the suffering Gevaudanois, nothing could have been further from the truth. Heedless of royal pronouncements, the Beast continued its terrible ravages. As a result, many villages were virtually abandoned when their inhabitants fled to other districts to escape the Beast.

In the late winter and early spring of 1767 the situation in Le Gevaudan reached a climax of horror and fear. Daily the Beast stalked through the villages, staring in at the windows and attacking those unlucky enough to be caught out in the streets. So demoralized had the once brave peasants become, that none even dared fire at it, though it repeatedly presented itself as an open target.

Finally, in the month of June, after almost three years of terror, the Marquis d' Apcher – a nobleman living on the western edge of the ravaged area – organized an immense posse of several hundred men and resolved not to rest until the Beast had been killed.

Fanning out in circles through the brush-covered countryside, they drove their quarry into an ever-narrowing area. On the evening of June 19, the Marquis' huntsmen had the monster surrounded in a patch of open woods at Le Sogne d' Auvert. An old peasant, Jean Chastel, having loaded his musket with silver bullets – traditionally the only effective weapon against werewolves – had retired a little apart from the other hunters to read his prayer book when he saw the Beast advancing toward him.

Very calmly he closed the prayer book, took off his reading spectacles, aimed his musket and fired. The shot hit the Beast in the chest but it kept on coming. Chastel fired again. This time the silver bullet pierced the heart of the Beast, which fell dead at his feet.

His companions now ran up. Exclaiming with joy, they helped him lift up and examine the monstrous corpse that lay before them.

Exactly what they saw has been a matter of dispute ever since. In the first report made to the authorities several of the hunters are said to have remarked that the creature's peculiar feet, cropped ears and great size made it certain that it could not have been a wolf.

Nevertheless, a huge wolf carcass was paraded triumphantly through Le Gevaudan for two weeks. Then it was packed up in a case to be sent to Versailles as proof that the Beast had at last actually been killed. The carcass soon started to putrefy in the mid-summer heat and had been carried only a small part of the long journey to Versailles when it became necessary to bury it.

To compound the mystery the official records fail – deliberately or otherwise – to name the precise spot at which this wolf, whether really the Beast or not, was buried. In contrast, the place where Chastel shot the monster is still well known and always pointed out to tourists. The grass there has a reddish tinge and, according to local superstition, is never cropped by animals.

A few miles away at the parsonage of St. Martin-de-Bouchaux you can see the double-barreled gun, with its carved butt decorated with a silver plate bearing Chastel's name, from which the silver bullets were fired that killed the Beast. It was at this parsonage a half-century ago that the late Abbe Pourcher compiled a thick volume presenting the details, collected by him from the municipal and clerical records throughout Le Gevaudan, of each of the murders committed by the monster.

Though the Abbe was unable to offer any proof of the mysterious creature's true nature, he wished to bring the facts regarding it to public attention, especially in view of the misstatements made by Robert Louis Stevenson, in the 1880s, in his *Travels with a Donkey*.

Traversing Le Gevaudan hurriedly, Stevenson picked up a garbled impression of the Beast from the tales told around tavern firesides, over a century after the event. He failed to clarify his picture by what seems to have been some sketchy background reading done afterward, mainly in an obscure historical novel on the subject by Elie Berthet. Stevenson describes the Beast as "the Napoleon of wolves ... living 10 months" (actually almost three years) "at free quarters in Gevaudan and Vivarais ... it ate shepherdesses celebrated for their beauty, pursued armed horsemen, and was seen at noonday chasing a post coach and outrider, on the highroad, the latter fleeing at a gallop.

"The Beast was placarded like a political offender, and 10,000 francs offered for his pelt;" Stevenson continued, "and yet it was only a common wolf ... "

This statement cannot be supported by any official records, in spite of the anti-climactic exhibition of a wolf carcass purporting to be that which Chastel shot. There is more than a suggestion in official records that the truth about Chastel's real victim was too hideous to reveal publicly; that a wolf had to be hurriedly substituted as something concrete to prove that the weird killings at last had come to an end.

What was the Beast of Le Gevaudan then?

Was it actually a werewolf or vampire, one of the terrible undead who prey on the blood of the living and are vulnerable only to the silver bullets of superstitious legend?

Could the Beast have been an enormously powerful and sadistic maniac dressed in animal costume?

After the lapse of two centuries and with the vital evidence of the exact description of the creature shot by Chastel probably lost forever, no certain answer can be given.

The last-named possibility, however, seems most consistent with the known facts; particularly when it is remembered that the Auvergne area was noted during the Middle Ages for its sorcerers, some of whom allegedly turned themselves into wolves at will. The strange Beast may have been a last, crazed inheritor of this tradition, slaking his sadistic blood-lust with the ripped-out hearts of hundreds of Gevaudanois children.

> *Even a man who is pure at heart,*
> *and says his prayers by night,*
> *may become a wolf when the wolfbane blooms*
> *and the autumn moon is bright.*
> *– The Wolf Man, 1941*

FATE October 1961

ANIMAL TERROR IN THE FRENCH COUNTRYSIDE
Loren Coleman

Beginning in June 1764, the forests and fields of a region in southeastern France, the Gevaudan, saw an unparalleled terror.

One woman said that as she was taking care of her cattle she was attacked by a horrible animal, the size of a donkey or cow, looking somewhat like a very large wolf. Luckily, her cattle chased it away.

Soon, children started disappearing and their mutilated bodies, along with those of young men and women, began to be found. In July of that year, the first victim — a little girl — was discovered with her heart ripped from her body. The discovery plunged the countryside into horror.

In late 1764 *The Paris Gazette* described in detail what became known as the "Beast of Gevaudan." It was "much higher than a wolf, low before, and his feet are armed with talons. His hair is reddish, his head large, and the muzzle of it is shaped like that of a greyhound; his ears are small and straight; his breast is wide and gray; his back streaked with black; his large mouth is provided with sharp teeth."

Fearing a *loup-garou,* a werewolf, bands of men roamed the Gevaudan, searching and dispatching all manner of animals. More than a hundred wolves were shot, but the brutal murders continued.

Terrifying close encounters and reports of the seeming inability of bullets to harm the Beast only reinforced the notion that something supernatural was attacking the children. During 1766, whole villages would be abandoned if the Beast was sighted nearby. A huge wolf was killed at one point, but the massacre of innocents did not stop.

The Beast of Gevaudan terrorizes the French countryside.

Finally, in June 1767, stimulated by a huge reward, a massive hunt was organized by the Marquis d'Apcher. Hundreds of professional hunters were divided into small groups. On June 17, the Beast charged one of these small hunting parties, and Jean Chastel, armed with a gun loaded with silver bullets, killed the animal with a shot directly to the heart. It was said that when the beast was cut open, the clavicle of a girl was found in its stomach.

The toll of lives during the Beast's rampage was estimated at between 60 and 100, but the Beast itself was finally dead. Its rotting carcass was paraded around the region for two weeks and then buried someplace in the countryside.

For chroniclers of these events – whether they be mammalogists, cryptozoologists, folklorists, or werewolfologists – there seemed no hope that the mystery of this animal's identity could ever be solved – until recently.

Speculation about the Beast's nature has been rife. Some – like Michel Meurger in Fortean Studies #1 – called it a murky legend. Meurger states, "The identification of the scourge of Gevaudan with a hyena was as weak as the one with a panther. Both were traditional." And, "The hyena and leopard from 1764-1766 were, like dragons, the stuff of folklore."

Meurger's thesis was that it was all just a folktale based on sightings of wolves. Then, during the summer of 1997, a rumor circulated that the fur of the Beast killed by Chastel had been rediscovered in the collections of the Museum National d'Histoire Naturelle in Paris. Had scientists made a great find, a physical piece of evidence of the devilish Beast which could be subjected to a DNA test? Would this 1997 discovery end the mystery?

Franz Jullien, a taxidermist at the museum, stated that while a stuffed specimen of the Beast may have been in the museum collections from 1766 to 1819, as the rumor suggests, the contemporary discovery was merely a long-lost manuscript. Based on contemporary descriptions and comparisons, it identified the specimen as a striped hyena. This solution to had previously been proposed by novelist Henri Pourrat and naturalist Garard Manatory, based on historical accounts.

So what of the motives behind the killings? Jean Chastel's son Antoine was said to have lived as a hermit on Mount Mouchet (still untouched forest today), with a menagerie of beasts, including a hyena. Cryptozoologist Michel Raynal and I have both speculated that Antoine Chastel might have used this animal to attack the young boys and girls, who were all Catholics (surprising in this region, which is home to a lot of Protestants).

What can be said is that when Jean killed the beast, it seemed to recognize him (strange indeed!), and that there were no killings when Antoine was prisoner for three months (because of some problems with the soldiers of King Louis XV) in the prison of Saugues. The attacks resumed when he was liberated, and stopped only when Jean Chastel killed the animal, which turned out to be a hyena.

The 1997 discovery has really only raised more questions. What if the Chastels had merely designed a clever plan to gain a quick fortune? Why in the midst of the hundreds of hunters, was it the father of the menagerie owner who would be in the right place at the right time to kill the Beast? What if the wrong beast was killed?

Who is to say what the Beast of Gevaudan really was? Was it a striped hyena from Africa? A form of aggressive hairy hominid? Or the cover for a serial killer? And will we ever know?

The enigma of the Beast of Gevaudan remains just that... a riddle unsolved in our mysterious world.

Loren Coleman: Cryptozoologist, author, former FATE *columnist,* FATE *contributor.*

FATE March 1998

MEN INTO WEREWOLVES
Otto Burma

Little Marie Bidel heard a small noise in the brush behind her as she sat playing with her doll at the foot of a tree in a woods near the village of Naizan in the Jura Mountains in 1584. She turned to see branches pulled back by hairy paw-like hands. In horror, she stared into a hideous, snarling face which was neither animal nor human but somehow both, with hairy skin and long sharp teeth. Marie knew at once – because of stories she had heard – that the monster was a *loup- garou*, werewolf!

She jumped back screaming for her brother, Benoist, 16, who was up in the tree gathering fruit. As the monster moved toward her, young Benoist, with knife in hand, leaped from the tree and fell on the werewolf's back. But the creature was too agile for the boy and in an instant, twisted free, tearing the knife from his hand. They rolled over and over on the ground, the werewolf clawing at the boy's throat with its fangs.

The screams of little Marie brought neighbors to the scene. Surprised and enraged, the group of peasants attacked the werewolf and killed it. They then turned their attention to Benoist, who was bleeding profusely from the throat. Helplessly they watched the boy die. When they turned their attention again to the body of the werewolf, they were amazed to find in its place the nude body of a girl recognized as Pernette Gandillon.

A huge werewolf eats a girl.

When the peasants returned to their villages with this strange story, there was an official investigation. This led to the arrest of others of Pernette's family. In prison, the Gandillons acted as if they were possessed, walking on all fours and howling like wild beasts. They lost all resemblance to humanity; their eyes turned red and gleaming, their hair matted, their teeth became long and sharp, and their fingernails turned horny and claw-like.

The Gandillon family was personally examined by the great jurist Henri Boguet, Judge of Saint-Claude in the Jura Mountains, and he reported the case in his book, *Discours des Sorciers*, published in 1610. That this story cannot be dismissed as the product of superstitious peasants and a gullible judge, is indicated by other well documented accounts of werewolves in France.

Jean Grenier

The case of Jean Grenier, the madman who thought he was a werewolf, is recorded by Pierre de Lancre, a noted jurist and judges of Bordeaux. It can be found in his *L'Inconstance*, published in 1612.

On May 29, 1603, several people reported that they had been attacked or had seen others attacked by a large wolf in the district of Roche Chalais. Among them was a girl named Margaret Poiret who claimed that she was attacked by a young man named Jean Grenier who had appeared in the form of a wolf.

The court collected a formidable array of detailed information concerning the many attacks. The victims and witnesses all swore that they had seen only an enormous wolf. When Jean Grenier was brought in, he confessed proudly that he was a werewolf and proceeded to related countless details of the crimes which he could have known only had he been the one who committed them.

It was thoroughly established that the victims had been attacked by a wolf and that Grenier had been present at each of the attacks. The court refused to believe that werewolves existed, but if werewolves did not exist, then either the witnesses or Jean Grenier must be mad. There was only one solution: Jean Grenier was declared insane by the court and committed to the Monastery of the Cordeliers in Bordeaux for life.

In 1610, after Grenier had been at the monastery for seven years, Lancre visited him there. Lancre describes Grenier as having glittering, deep-set eyes, long, black fingernails, and sharp, protruding teeth. He walked on all fours with greater ease than he walked upright.

Grenier confessed to Lancre that he had been a werewolf but had given up the practice. Nevertheless, he stated that he still craved human flesh, especially the flesh of little girls, and he hoped that it would not be long before he could taste it again.

Jacques Roulet

A similar case is that of Jacques Roulet, the werewolf of Caude. He was tried and condemned at Angers in 1598.

At a desolate spot near Caude, Symphorien Damon, archer of a provost's company, found the mangled and bloody corpse of a 15-year-old boy. As he approached the body in company with some peasants, three wolves fled into the woods. Giving chase, Damon and the peasants suddenly came upon a half-naked man with a long beard and long hair. His hands were covered with blood and under his claw-like nails they found shreds of human flesh. This was Jacques Roulet.

He confessed that he had been one of the wolves who had killed the youth (whose name it was learned was Cornier) and that he was able to transform himself into a wolf by means of a salve. Although condemned to death by the court of Angers, he was eventually committed as insane to the hospital of Saint-Germain-des-Pres.

Beast of Gevaudan

During the years 1764-1765, an alleged werewolf spread terror throughout all of France. This was the "Wild Beast of Gevaudan" reported in the *London Magazine,* January 1765. This monster was seen by hundreds of people who reported it as the most terrible of all *loups-garous.* A large reward was offered to anyone who could kill it. A detachment of dragoons was sent out to hunt it down but the monster would attack even armed groups. It is reported to have devoured over 100 persons. There is no satisfactory report that it was ever captured.

The case of Francis Bertrand, in 1849, was one of the most famous of modern times and served as the basis of Guy Endore's novel, *The Werewolf of Paris.* Bertrand habitually dug up the dead bodies of women buried in Paris cemeteries and tore them to pieces. He was never seen in the form of a wolf – in fact, he was never seen at all though the cemeteries were heavily guarded by men and dogs. He was eventually captured in a Paris hospital where he had gone to get treatment for wounds inflicted by a spring-gun mounted on one of the graves he molested.

Uttenheim Werewolf

In November 1925, a large wolf was seen on the streets of the village of Uttenheim, near Strasburg, in the Vosges Mountains of Alsace. In sight of the whole village, it was shot and killed by the village policeman. When the crowd reached the body, they discovered it to be that of a young man of the village. The policeman was charged with murder but on the testimony of numerous eye-witnesses he was cleared. It was learned at the trial that the young man had been heard to boast that he could change into a wolf at will. The news of this trial was carried in all the

French newspapers of the time and is reported in Montague Summers' book *The Werewolf.*

Explanations

The evidence for werewolfism is convincing enough to lead many learned men to attempt to explain it. One explanation offered is that an actual physical transformation takes place. This would mean that there is a change in the cells of the body which causes the human form to assume more or less the appearance of a wolf. It should be noted that this change is seldom described as complete. The werewolf apparently does not lose all its human characteristics. For instance, it usually does not have a tail, its hands become hairy and claw-like but do not become paws, and its face resembles more an ape than a wolf. However, some werewolves have been said to make drastic physical changes.

It has been demonstrated that concentration or auto-suggestion can cause changes in body cells. Thought has been shown to be capable of removing blemishes and excess fat. Dr. H.V. Allington, a noted California dermatologist, has reported that warts can be removed by auto-suggestion (FATE, April-May 1952). Meditation even can cause open wounds to appear on the skin, as is indicated by the cases of Therese Neumann (FATE, September 1950) and Padre Pio (FATE, November 1952). Dr. Pierre Janet caused a large blister to form on the skin of a hysterical girl by means of suggestion. There are many other cases which demonstrate that the body is subject to the mind. Thus, it is not too much to suppose that belief or auto-suggestion can lead to the radical physical changes characteristic of werewolves.

According to literature on the subject, it usually is necessary to go through some sort of ritual as a prelude to werewolfism. This apparently consists of drinking water from the footprint of a wolf, partaking of its brains, haunting the lair of a wolf, or wearing a girdle made of its skin. These rituals, together with the secret ointments sometimes used and the odor of the mysterious lycanthrope flower, probably increase the strength of auto-suggestion.

Even outright self-hypnosis may be involved. A person under hypnosis, for example, can be made to believe he is a wolf. In certain instances, it may not be so much a matter of belief as that hypnosis awakens parts of the brain which were dominant when man existed much lower on the scale of evolution than he does today. Many cases are known of individuals who have lapsed back to animal behavior – without the influence of any hypnosis.

William Seabrook, in his book *Witchcraft*, reports the case of a girl in a self-induced trance who gave a very convincing demonstration of wolf behavior. Dr. Milton V. Kline of the Westchester County Department of Health, New York State, conducted an experiment in which he suggested to a woman under hypnosis that she go back in time to a stage of life found only in her early ancestors. This woman knew little or nothing about animal psychology, yet she showed aspects of animal behavior which have been discovered only recently by animal psychologists. In the waking state, she was unable to reproduce this behavior or even to describe it.

Such evidently was not the case with the French woman in Africa who was kept in a cage by her husband. William Seabrook, who witnessed the incident, relates that the husband believed his wife to be a werewolf.

FATE September 1953

THE REINCARNATED WEREWOLF
Rosemary Ellen Guiley

One of the most unusual werewolf cases on record is the Anspach Werewolf of Anspach Germany, in which the werewolf was believed to be a despised deceased person who returned from the dead.

The incidents took place in 1685 in Anspach (now Ansbach), a principality in northern Bavaria, which was still under the rule of the Holy Roman Empire. A wolf began terrorizing the area. At first, it preyed upon livestock, tearing them to shreds and devouring parts of their bodies, leaving bloody bits of flesh behind. The wolf soon extended its killing to humans, stalking women and children.

The residents of Anspach were certain they were not dealing with an ordinary wolf, but with a werewolf. Furthermore, they believed this werewolf was their former Bürgermeister, a man who had been universally despised and who had recently died. He was coming back in the form of a marauding wolf to wreak havoc and revenge.

The Werewolf of Anspach is chased into a well, and its corpse dressed like the dead Bürgermeister and hung from a gibbet.

A great hunt was mounted. The hunters and their dogs flushed the wolf out of the forest and chased it. The wolf leaped into an uncovered well for refuge – which proved to be a fatal mistake. Trapped, it was easily slain by the hunters.

During those times, it was common for offending corpses to be paraded through town like trophies. Criminals, ravaging wolves and werewolves were put on display to assure the locals that they were now safe, and, in the case of human criminals, to warn others of the gruesome fate of lawbreakers.

The residents of Anspach wanted to lay the spirit of the Bürgermeister to rest forever. First, they paraded the carcass through the marketplace. Then they severed the dead wolf's muzzle and dressed the carcass up in flesh-colored men's clothing. Then they placed a wig, beard and mask on the mutilated head to represent the hated Bürgermeister. They hanged the costumed wolf on a gibbet for everyone to see. It was then taken down, preserved, and put on permanent display in the local museum, as evidence that werewolves really existed, and people should be fearful of them.

What eventually happened to the werewolf carcass is not known. The return of the Bürgermeister as a rampaging beast, consuming flesh and blood, also has overtones of the vampire, which escapes its grave to prey upon the living. In the case of the Anspach Werewolf, no effort was made to dig up the Bürgermeister to see is his corpse was in the "vampire condition." Perhaps vampire beliefs were not prevalent there. Werewolf beliefs certainly were strong. The locals were convinced the dead man had returned as a werewolf – making this a rare case of a "reincarnated werewolf."

THE STRANGE CASE OF THE WEREWOLF'S TEETH
Nicholas P. Warren

Have werewolves existed within historical times? Is it possible for evil behavior to be preordained by a hereditary curse? And what bearing does the lost science of alchemy have on both these questions? The case of the Hungarian Countess Elizabeth Bathory (1560 -1614) comes closest to posing these questions seriously, if not to actually answering them.

Countess Bathory (pronounced ba-TORY) is officially credited with the murder of 650 girls. A minimum estimate is 50. The official number may well be exaggerated since the prosecuting authorities had a vested interest in neutralizing Elizabeth, to whom the Crown owed enormous sums of unpaid debts. In any event, had she confined herself to peasant girls, instead of daughters of the nobility, she would not have incurred punishment at all.

The barbaric Vlad the Fifth (1431-1476), Crown Prince of Wallachia, is usually considered to be the model for *Dracula*. A very convincing case can, however, be made that the author of the original novel, Bram Stoker, was in fact inspired by Countess Bathory. Stoker borrowed heavily from an earlier novel, *Carmilla*, written in 1872 by Sheridan Le Fanu. Carmilla tells the story of a vampiric Austrian countess and it was written within seven years of the publication in English of an account of Elizabeth's exploits. Most interestingly, a canceled chapter of Stoker's own *Dracula* novel involves a vampiric countess from Syria in Austria.

Elizabeth herself resided at Csejthe (pronounced Cheyteh), then in Austria-Hungary but now in Czechoslovakia. The exact location is a castle, still extant but now in ruins, standing on the Vah River between the towns of Bratislava in Czechoslovakia and Esztergom in Hungary. The real countess had links with Transylvania; her cousin Stephan became prince of that territory in 1571.

The theory that Elizabeth was the original model for Dracula has been examined by Prof. Raymond McNally in his book *Dracula Was a Woman* (1983). It does seem to me, however, that the professor has made a number of errors in his treatise, not least of which is the statement that the countess' castle is in Transylvania, a territory once in Hungary but ceded to Romania after the First World War. Csejthe Castle actually stands 400 miles from Transylvania.

The crimes which earned Elizabeth Bathory this notoriety were the torture and murder of young girls to obtain their blood. Most of these murders were committed at Csejthe but some of them took place at a town house in Lobowitz Square in Vienna. This provides a further connection with the vampiric Austrian countess of Stoker's novel.

The countess wanted this blood in order to bathe in it and so obtain rejuvenation (again like the fictional Count Dracula). She was, therefore, known as a living vampire as opposed to the reanimated variety. And because she also bit the flesh of her victims she was called a werewolf. Indeed, it was as a werewolf that she first became known to the English-speaking world as "A Hungarian Bather in Blood" in *The Book of Werewolves*, published in London in 1865. Curiously, the author of this book, Sabine Baring-Gould (1834-1924), is far better known as a writer of hymns including "Onward Christian Soldiers."

We must now consider the connections between alchemy, werewolfism and a possible congenital curse. These connections are illustrated in the Bathory family crests, which I believe have never before been examined in this light.

In Elizabeth Bathory's time family crest showed alchemical symbol of dragon, Ouroboros. Three wolves' teeth linked by staff form "E," for Elizabeth.

The earliest relevant heraldic crest which I have been able to trace is of a direct ancestor, Sigimundus Bathory. This crest features three wolves' teeth surmounted by a crown and surrounded by the word NONONONONONON. This curious term is significant because it reads the same in either direction – that is, it is palindromic. In later years, its hidden meaning was to reveal itself.

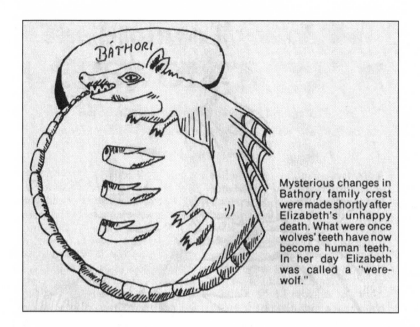

Mysterious changes in Bathory family crest were made shortly after Elizabeth's unhappy death. What were once wolves' teeth have now become human teeth. In her day Elizabeth was called a "were-wolf."

By Elizabeth's time, the family crest had been modified to allow us a true glimpse of what was in hand. The palindromic word has been replaced by the figure of a dragon biting its own tail and the three wolves' teeth have been linked by a staff to spell the letter E for Elizabeth. It appears as such on the countess' best-known portrait.

The overwhelming significance of the dragon motif is that it constitutes the most important and enduring symbol of alchemy, a lost science or art, which was still influential in 16th- and 17th-century Europe. Alchemists had two goals. The first was to discover the philosopher's stone (not necessarily a stone in the conventional sense, but rather a chemical precipitate) which could turn common metals into gold. The second goal was the *elixir vitae*, the secret of eternal youth. To Elizabeth Bathory, this was the blood of young girls. As a recent commentator stated, "She believed that blood was the elixir of youth."

The dragon that appears on Elizabeth's coat of arms is clearly the alchemical dragon, officially known as the Ouroboros, from the Greek, meaning tail-biter. It represents alchemy itself which begins and ends with the One, a fundamental substance (*prima materia*) from which the philosopher's stone might be derived. The Ouroboros is also a symbol for various candidates for the One, including the metal silver which was equated in alchemy with the moon, traditional controller of werewolf behavior.

There has always been an affinity, if not an actual connection, between alchemy and werewolves. It was said of one werewolf, for example, that "his depravity of mind led him by choice to the realms of black magic ritual and to the use of charms, potions and ointments."

Countess Elizabeth Bathory also served as model for another classic horror story, *Frankenstein*, written by Mary Shelley in 1816. Her hero was another seeker after the elixir of life and took his name from Baron Frankenstein who died in 1673. The baron lived at Castle Frankenstein close to Magnetenberg on the Rhine, near Darmstadt in Germany. There is no evidence, however, that the baron indulged in alchemy, unlike the countess who inherited not only an alchemical family crest but also a crippled dwarf for an assistant. While no dwarf appears in Mary Shelley's original novel, he features prominently as Igor in all later films.

The final alarming change in Elizabeth Bathory's family crest appears to have been made shortly after her death. And it is the last known version of the family coat of arms.

During the 16th and 17th centuries, alleged werewolves were still executed, particularly in Germany. The most famous execution was that of Peter Stump or Stubb at Cologne in 1589. His fate was shared by his wife and daughter who were burned at the stake to stamp out the evil of hereditary werewolfism.

Countess Elizabeth Bathory was possibly more fortunate. Her punishment was to be bricked up in her own quarters where she eventually died "without light and without God" three-and-a-half years later. Her accomplices were beheaded.

In the meantime, her family crest had undergone the most remarkable change, a change which remains unexplained. The three wolves' teeth were now human teeth. Judging by their roots they are human molars or possibly premolars which grind food but cannot tear or incise flesh.

We can only speculate on the meaning of this drastic change.

FATE June 1986

WITCHES, WEREWOLVES, AND MADNESS
Charles A. Coulombe

By necessity practical and by philosophy stem, these folk were not beautiful in their sins.
Erring as all mortals must, they were forced by their rigid code to seek concealment above all else; so that they came to use less and less taste in what they concealed.

– H.P. Lovecraft, The Picture in the House

ew England has always held a large part of our national consciousness in its claw. Thanksgiving, the Pilgrim Fathers, the Boston Tea Party, Bunker Hill – all of these are cherished icons to virtually every American. Does not the archetypal Christmas scene feature a snow-covered New England village, with its white-spired Congregational church? What about Fourth of July picnics, and "Ye Olde Shoppes?" These, too, find their inspiration in New England.

But beneath this idyllic surface runs a darker stream. The Puritan inheritance of guilt and repression, of secret sin and public virtue, has left its mark upon the region. Such writers as Nathaniel Hawthorne and H. P. Lovecraft wrote eloquently of the effects of this inheritance. Trapped between the fearful righteousness of the Calvinists and the terrors supposedly wrought by the devil's minions, many an early Puritan must have agreed with Hawthorne's character in *Young Goodman Brown*: "There is no good on Earth; and sin is but a name. Come, devil! For to thee is this world given!"

Lovecraft wrote: "All these things conspired to produce an environment in which the black whisperings of sinister grandams were heard far beyond the chimney comer, and in which tales of witchcraft and unbelievable secret monstrosities lingered long after the dread days of the Salem nightmare."

We have all heard of Salem and its witches, of course, and we think we know about the supposed judicial murder of innocent victims there in 1692. But do we? Was the witchcraft practiced at Salem a delusion? Not so, says historian Chadwick Hansen in his 1969 study, *Witchcraft at Salem*: "While it is clearly true that the majority of persons executed for witchcraft were innocent, it is equally true that some of them, in Massachusetts and elsewhere, were guilty."

Hansen, using the original records and making comparisons with other cases, argues that witchcraft was indeed being practiced at Salem by a few of those accused of it. He contends that the use of images to cast baleful spells against people worked because its victims believed that it would; the resulting hysteria led to the innocent suffering with the guilty. If his contentions are correct, our whole understanding of the affair must be revised, as must for what we know of New England as a whole. From the execution of Anne Hibbins in 1656 to the revolution, it seemed that the region was alive with witchcraft. Every hamlet had its old crone, who practiced her craft at the edge of town; whether executed or (far more often) suffered to live on to extreme old age, her legend lingered long after.

Some locations in New England had more witches than others; in some of these, witchcraft was not the only thing to be feared. One such place is the now deserted village of Dogtown, between Gloucester and Rockport on the Cape Anne peninsula. Here lived old Luce George, a wild-eyed hag, and her niece, Tammy Younger, who so bewitched the oxen hauling grain past their cabin that the animals stood with lolling tongues and would not move until part of their load had been donated to the devil, as represented by Luce George. Here, too, dwelt young Judy Rhines, casting her spells over fine strong lads; and old Peg Wesson, who, in the guise of a black crow, followed a detachment of soldiers to Louisburg in 1745 and annoyed them until the crow was shot by a silver bullet made from the buttons of a soldier's coat. That very moment, back in Gloucester, Old Peg fell down, broke her leg, and soon died – some say with a silver bullet in her.

Witchcraft is not the only horror for which Dogtown was noted. It was rumored also that some of the folk of the shunned village were werewolves. Sightings of huge wolf-like animals over the years might be dismissed as myth were it not for the fact that such sightings continue to be made by reliable witnesses today.

A werewolf attacks a woman.

Robert Ellis Cahill, former sheriff of Salem, said one sighting was reported by a David Myska of Allston, Massachusetts, on March 17, 1984. At 6:00 P.M. that day, as the full moon was rising over the sand dunes across the Annisquam river at Crane's Beach Reservation, Myska saw a large animal roaming the cliffs above the dunes.

Myska reported to the Ipswich police that it was a very large dog or cat, possibly a mountain lion, but it was "too big to be a wolf or coyote." It's been two centuries since a cougar has been sighted in Eastern Massachusetts.

Four nights later, one of the reservation's deer was found dead with a slashed throat and deep fang marks in its head and chest. Ipswich animal control officer Harry Leno declared that "it was horribly mutilated, yet no part of it had been eaten." The deer's killer was "an animal thirsting for blood."

That same evening across the Annisquam at Raynard street, two teenagers saw "a gray monstrous dog-like animal, running into the woods. It had big teeth and was foaming at the mouth," Cahill said. "The people who live on Raynard Street remain a bit squeamish about the strange animal. For, you see, Raynard Street leads into Dogtown, and Dogtown overlooks Crane's Beach Reservation, and…well, as Harry Leno says, 'anything is possible.'"

Werewolves are not the only creatures believed to have bedeviled New Englanders. Reports of vampirism are not unknown. In 1854, a Connecticut newspaper, *The Norwich Courier*, reported some odd goings-on in the town of Jewett. In 1846, or 1847, Griswold native Horace Ray died of tuberculosis (in those days called consumption). Two of his sons developed the same disease and followed him in death, the last and younger dying in 1852.

When a third son was diagnosed with the same illness, it was decided to dig up the two deceased brothers and cremate them, because the dead were thought to be feeding on the living. If the bodies were allowed to remain whole, people thought they would continue to do so. Family and friends descended upon the cemetery on June 8, 1854, dug up the corpses, built a huge fire, and burned them on the spot. In a similar incident 20 years later, William Rose of Placedale, Rhode Island, exhumed the body of his daughter and burned her heart, in the belief that she was feeding off remaining family members' vitality.

In October 1890, the *Boston Transcript* reported a famous case of vampirism that had shocked the town of Woodstock, Vermont, some 50 years earlier. At that time, four local doctors gathered on the Green to burn the heart of a tuberculosis victim named Corwin in an iron pot. The whole town convened to watch the proceedings: The organ was consumed by flames and the pot was buried in a hole dug 15 feet deep into the Green. A granite bolder was set on top, the Green was reseeded, and the spot was sprinkled with bull's blood.

The unfortunate Mr. Corwin's brother was made to eat some of the ashes, likewise mixed with bull's blood. It seems that after his brother died, the surviving Corwin also fell ill with tuberculosis, and he claimed his brother visited him each night to suck his blood. His physician, Dr. Joseph Gallup, ordered the unorthodox remedy. At the exhumation, the good doctor found that "the vampire's heart contained its victim's blood."

Exeter and Wickford, Rhode Island, also faced their share of goings-on, starting in 1883. Once again, tuberculosis was involved. On December 8, 1883, Mary Brown died in Exeter of the disease. Six months later, one of her seven daughters – also named Mary – fell victim to tuberculosis. Five years after that, the family's only son Edwin contracted the same malady.

Fearful of following his mother and sister to the grave, he left his farm in West Wickford and moved to the Colorado Rockies. Not a year had passed, however, before he received the news that his 19-year-old sister Mercy had perished of tuberculosis. Convinced that there was more at work than sickness, he returned home to Rhode Island to do battle with whatever was decimating his family.

Certain that a vampire was at work, and wishing to follow the old-time New England cure, he had all three bodies exhumed. His mother and Mary were skeletons; but Mercy, dead for two months, was as fresh as the day she was buried. The attending physician found whole blood in her heart. There, beside her burial plot in Chestnut Hill cemetery, her brother Edwin reburied her now-heartless body. He burned the organ, then ate the cooked muscle. Sadly for him, the remedy did not work – he died a few weeks later.

Many other odd events have occurred in this part of the country. Along the lower slopes of Mt. Riga, near Salisbury, Connecticut, for several days and nights in November 1802, three houses in Sage's Ravine were battered with mortar pieces and rocks. None of the missiles came from the area, and although they shattered windows, the rocks did not fly through the rooms but settled carefully on the adjoining window sills. Despite careful vigilance, no assailant was ever found. In Cornwall, Connecticut, on State Highway 4 near Cornwall Bridge, is the footpath to Dark Entry, a deserted hillside covered with hemlock, pine, and laurel. In 1871 only one family lived in the deep woods there. The husband left for two days to pick up supplies in the village. When he returned, his wife was stark-raving mad. She was unable to tell him what horror had frightened her out of her wits.

A similar incident occurred in Dudleytown, likewise in the Town of Cornwall. Now a ghost town, the community was founded in the 1630s by four brothers, Abijah, Bazvillai, Abviel, and Gideon Dudley (all of whom died unpleasant deaths). Dudleytown was at first as normal a settlement as a Puritan village could be. But strangeness soon prevailed. A prominent physician, Dr. William Tanner, built a beautiful mansion for himself and his wife. He returned from a few days' trip to New York to find that his wife had gone mad.

The neighbors told Tanner that she fled the house, screaming that ghosts and "animal-like creatures" were pursuing her. Shaken, the doctor's mind gave way completely when a man named Gersham Hollister was found brutally murdered at the Tanner house. Babbling about demons and ghosts, Tanner maintained until his own death that Hollister had been dispatched by some strange beast.

In the face of these and similar incidents, people left Dudleytown in droves. By 1892, only one family remained – the Brophys. John Brophy declared in public that he would not be driven from his home by any ghosts or wild animals. But that year Mrs. Brophy died suddenly; a few weeks later his two little children vanished and were never found again. A week after the children disappeared, the house burned to the ground.

John Brophy wandered into Cornwall raving about green spirits and animals with cloven hooves who had tried to capture him. Since then, no one has lived in Dudleytown, and it preserves its eerie reputation. Sheriff Cahill writes about Dudleytown: "Today, I know of no ghost hunter who would dare to spend the night among the ruins of Connecticut's notorious ghost town, and, as for me, I wouldn't visit Dudleytown again even in daylight hours."

Cornwall is far from the only tucked-away corner of New England to have such a reputation for evil. Inhuman agents were not solely to blame for such reputations. In out-of-the-way spots such as Seabrook Village on the New Hampshire coast and the ill-favored central Massachusetts hamlets of Enfield, Prescott, and Dana (now perhaps mercifully buried beneath the waters of the Quabbin reservoir), isolation, strange cults, and inbreeding were commonplace.

The W.P.A. *Guide to New Hampshire* said, "A section of the town of Seabrook speaks a language strangely reminiscent of rural England and at times suggestive of the Yorkshire dialect .... Many manners and customs of early days are retained." Until fairly recently, such a cheerful interpretation could well be supplemented almost word for word by this description of early 19th-century Enfield as "a narrow scanty valley, of sterile hillsides, its people devoid of culture, their schools inferior, their religion a somber Calvinism, intemperance, and immorality prevalent in the back districts."

The religious yearnings of such folk often took strange and horrifying forms; much valuable information regarding several cults of this type may be found in an essay by FATE contributor Andrew E. Rothovius, "Lovecraft and the New England Megaliths" (in *The Dark Brotherhood and Other Pieces*, August Derleth, ed., Arkham House, 1967). Rothovius described one of the most frightening of these cults: "In [the late 1770s], a strange forerunner of the Transcendentalist movement flared up briefly at Harvard, down the Nashoba River from Petersham .... Led by Shadrach Ireland, who had come from Charlestown with the woman he called his 'soul mate,' Abigail Lougee, it was a reaction to the aridities of the prevailing Calvinism, but with overtones suggesting that it drew on some survivals of the witch-cult that had gone underground after Salem, a century previously.

Calling itself the Brethren of the New Light, it advocated celibacy, mutual confession of sins, and a withdrawal from the 'people of the world,' who were soon to be done away with anyway, by the 'powers from outside.' The elect, however-i.e. the members of the cult-would then attain bodily immortality in the flesh. Those who died before needed to have their bodies preserved on platforms of stone, from whence they would arise, living and breathing, when the hour struck."

When Mother Ann Lee – the "Female Christ" – and her Shakers came to Harvard in 1781, they absorbed the New Light manifestation and did away with its more outrageous attributes. The putrefying remains of Ireland himself, who had died a few months earlier, were removed from a stone platform in the cellar of the house in which he had resided, and were given a decent burial in a nearby cornfield.

So it was, and, perhaps it still is. For although people from all over the world have come to live in New England, the ethos of the first Puritan settlers retains its dominance. Those shadows remain to haunt the imagination of a future Hawthorne, a Lovecraft, or a Stephen King. When you visit New England to watch the leaves turn, or enjoy a clambake, or walk Boston's Freedom Trail, keep your wits about you. You don't know what might be lurking.

Charles Coulombe: Writer and lecturer on religious, political, historical and literary topics.

FATE December 1996

FROM WEREWOLVES WITH LOVE: THE HISTORY OF VALENTINE'S DAY

Brad Steiger

Everyone thinks they know the origin of Valentine's Day. According to the most commonly accepted story, Emperor Claudius of Rome issued a decree forbidding marriage in the year 271. Roman generals had found that married men did not make very good soldiers, because they wanted to return as quickly as possible to their wives and children – and they didn't want to leave them to fight the emperor's battles in the first place. So Claudius issued his edict that there should be no more marriages, and all single men should report for duty.

A priest named Valentine deemed such a decree an abomination, and he secretly continued to marry young lovers. When Claudius learned of this extreme act of disobedience to his imperial command, he ordered the priest dragged off to prison and had him executed on February 14.

Father Valentine, the friend of sweethearts, became a martyr to love and the sanctity of marriage, and when the Church gained power in the Roman Empire, the Holy See was quick to make him a saint.

The early Church fathers were well aware of the popularity of a vast number of heathen gods and goddesses, as well as the dates of observation of pagan festivals, so they set about replacing as many of the entities and the holidays as possible with ecclesiastical saints and feast days. Mid-February had an ancient history of being devoted to acts of love of a far more passionate and lusty nature than the Church wished to bless, and the bishops moved as speedily as possible to claim the days of February 14 through 17 as belonging to Saint Valentine, the courageous martyr to the ties that bound couples in Christian love.

February Is for mating

Actually, there is no proof that the good priest Valentine even existed.

Some scholars trace the period of mid-February as a time for mating back to ancient Egypt. On those same days of the year that contemporary lovers devote to St. Valentine, men and women of the Egyptian lower classes determined their marital partners by the drawing of lots.

But the time of coupling that comes with the cold nights in February before the spring thaw likely had its true origin very near where Valentine supposedly met his demise.

Among the ancient Greeks and Romans, the Wolf Charmer was called the Lupicinus. Perhaps hearkening back to prehistoric times, the Lupicinus may well have been an individual tribesman who had a particular affinity for communicating with wolves. As the tribes developed agriculture and small villages, it was necessary to have a person skilled in singing with the wolves and convincing them not to attack their domesticated animals. The Lupicinus had the ability to howl with the wolves and lead them away from the livestock pens. In some views, because he also wore the pelt of a wolf, the Lupicinus also had the power to transform himself into a wolf if he so desired.

Rites of the Lupercalia

The annual Lupercali festival of the Romans on February 15 was a perpetuation of the ancient blooding rites of the hunter in which the novice is smeared with the blood of his first kill. The sacrificial slaying of a goat – representing the flocks that nourished early humans in their efforts to establish permanent dwelling places – was followed by the sacrifice of a dog, the watchful protector of a flock that would be the first to be killed by attacking wolves.

The blood of the she-goat and the dog were mixed, and a bloodstained knife was dipped into the fluid and drawn slowly across the foreheads of two noble-born children. Once the children had been "blooded," the gore was wiped off their foreheads with wool that had been dipped in goat milk. As the children were being cleansed, they were expected to laugh, thereby demonstrating their lack of fear of blood and their acknowledgment that they had received the magic of protection against wolves and wolfmen.

The god Lupercus, represented by a wolf, would next inspire and command men to behave as wolves, to act as werewolves during the festival.

Lupus (wolf) itself is not an authentic or original Latin word, but was borrowed from the Sabine dialect. Luperca, the she-wolf who suckled Romulus and Remus, may have given rise to secret fraternities known as the Luperci, who sacrificed she-goats at the entrances to their "wolves' dens." For centuries, the Luperci observed an annual ritual of chasing women through the streets of Roman cities and beating them with leather thongs.

Scholars generally agree that such a violent expression of eroticism celebrated the ancient behavior of primitive hunting tribes corralling captive women. Once a wolf man had ensnared a woman with his whip or thong, he would lead her away to be his wife or lover for as long as the "romance" lasted. Perhaps, as some scholars theorize, this yearly rite of lashing at women and lassoing them with leather thongs became a more acceptable substitute for the blood lust of the Luperci's latent werewolfism that in days past had seen them tearing the flesh of innocent victims with their teeth.

As the Romans grew ever more sophisticated, the Lupercali would be celebrated by a man binding the lady of his choice wrist to wrist, and later by passing a billet to his object of desire, suggesting a romantic rendezvous in some secluded place.

Christian marriage

One can easily see why the early Church fathers much preferred the union of man and woman to be smiled upon by St. Valentine, rather than the leering wolf god Lupercus. And, of course, they encouraged a knot tied securely by the sacred rite of marriage and blessed by the priest, rather than a fleeting midnight liaison.

By the Middle Ages, the peasantry in England, Scotland, and parts of France honored St. Valentine, but their customs seemed very much to hearken back to ancient Egypt and Rome. On the evening before Valentine's Day, the young people would gather in a village meeting place and draw names by chance. Each young woman would write her name or make her mark on a bit of cloth and place it into a large urn. Then each of the young men would draw a slip. The girl whose name or mark was on the piece of cloth became his sweetheart for the year.

This method of celebrating St. Valentine's Day quite often led to circumstances and situations that encouraged long-term and lasting relationships, blessed by the recital of marriage vows in the local church. If the young couple did not take the necessary steps to become bound in a church-sanctioned union, the parents of the respective "bride" and "groom" would actively arrange for the marriage sacrament to be observed.

It wasn't long before the peasant method of utilizing St. Valentine's Day to guarantee the next generation of field hands, construction workers, and merchants reached the ears of the upper classes, and the custom became popular among the young men and women of the aristocracy and the landed gentry. Since the prospect of arranged marriages between successful families meant far more to the upper classes in Europe than to the peasantry, parental supervision most often limited the interaction between their children to be "sweethearts" during Valentine's Day parties. By the late 1400s, the upper classes of Europe and England would come together in homes to celebrate Valentine's Day and allow their young men to draw a "valentine" with the name of a member of the opposite sex, beside whom he would be seated at a lavish dinner party. Hostesses took advantage of the holiday theme to express the tradition in colorful decorative schemes.

Gradually, Valentine's Day came to be synonymous with the exchange of pretty sentiments, written in flourishes on scented paper and decorated with hearts, arrows, doves, and cupids – those little pagan deities maintaining their hold on the ancient holiday. By the early 1800s, young men were taking care to create symbols of their passion on elaborate cards that they could offer to "My Valentine."

Today's customs

By the 1850s, Valentine's Day cards were being manufactured and sold commercially in England, and the custom of observing the holiday with cards to one's sweetheart became popular in the United States in the 1860s, around the time of the Civil War.

Today, of course, we have vast commercial enterprises centered around St. Valentine's Day, insisting that callow young men and seasoned husbands must buy their sweetheart a box of candy, a dozen roses, a diamond ring or necklace, or at least a five-dollar card. But don't let the slick advertisers fool you with all this talk of a saint named Valentine who was martyred for love. Remember that it all began with a hyped-up wolfman smeared in blood chasing the object of his desire with a leather thong.

One last word of advice: Forget the whip and stick with flowers and candy.

Brad Steiger: Author of numerous books and articles on the paranormal.

FATE February 2006

WEREWOLVES IN THE MODERN WORLD

PHANTOM WOLF
J.P.J. Chapman

Even now the West Country of England is host to superstition, witchcraft, magic and strange happenings of all kinds. Most of the villages have their own grey lady, headless horse and local witch.

The village of Pareham where I lived was no exception and often as a boy I listened with popping eyes to stories of the phantom wolf. These stories told how, on certain nights, the wolf howled around the village and could be seen loping in the moonlight along the Green Walk which led from my home to a gardener's cottage at the edge of the wood.

One of the older men of the village, a jovial fellow named Tapp, assured me that in his father's day the wolf had been shot in the leg and next day old Amy Prouse, a witch who had lived in the next village, was seen to be limping. When questioned about her bandaged leg she said she had cut it while chopping wood!

Tapp also said that, as a small girl, Amy had been seen collecting certain herbs from the hedges. When asked why she had replied, "I'm picking victuals for mother's toads." Her mother had been the wise woman of the nearby village of Aston. Tapp had gone to see her about his warts and she certainly knew how to get rid of them – with the orange-colored juice of an herb which grows freely in Somerset. He had found her cottage a fascinating place. Bunches of dried herbs hung from the old oak beams. Dried toads, pots of powdered snake skin and bags of charred feathers lay on shelves. On the mantle over the wide, open hearth stood many curious clay figures. Hanging within the chimney itself, so wide that one could peer up and see the sky, was an assortment of dried animal hearts stuck with pins. The local chimney sweep vouched for the truth of this also as these mysteries were taken down and carefully placed aside when he swept the chimney.

Love charms and ceremonies were part of the old lady's strange trade. One such ceremony included piercing the dry shoulder blade of a rabbit with a needle. It was to be pierced nine times and each time the following jingle was recited:

> *This bone I do not mean to prick*
> *but through my true love's heart I mean to stick*
> *and may he neither rest nor sleep*
> *until he comes to me and speaks.*

The bone was then burnt in the fire and results eagerly anticipated.

Beauty treatments were part of her stock-in-trade. And truly she and her daughter, Amy, had marvelous complexions that with the years did not turn sere and yellow and were remarkably free of wrinkles. To this day there is a recipe for one of her beauty masks used in the village.

Through the years I questioned many people in the village and it seemed that Amy Prouse and the phantom wolf were, in some way, connected. Tapp was convinced that she had been able to turn herself into a wolf when it suited her. Of course, she had been dead for many years now and why she should walk as a wolf was a mystery. But, according to many people, walk she did and always as a wolf. Those who saw this wolf swore that it was so powerful it even could cross water by walking on the surface.

I was told that the wolf loped across many miles of country, through valleys and glens, from the village of Aston, where Amy Prouse had lived, to the Green Walk near my home. I was particularly fond of this part of the garden. During good summer weather my friend, Tom Turner, and I often camped out there. It was a delightful spot of wide, grass-grown walk between overhanging oak trees and not in the least bit eerie. At the end of the Walk stood an old thatched, whitewashed cottage with a tangled, overgrown garden. It had not been occupied for many years for the village people swore that the water in the nearby well was bad. The old well-head was overgrown with brambles and the gear above it had long since disappeared.

The last gardener to live in this cottage had been Ted Prouse, a distant cousin of Amy's. He had been a queer, miserly chap who lived alone with only his old collie dog, Nelly, for company. Nelly had disappeared mysteriously one evening. She was never found and a few weeks later Ted had died.

Tapp told me that Amy had come over from Aston to clear up the cottage and take away the few bits of furniture. He remembered his father saying that she had made a great fuss at finding no money in the house and was worried because she could not find a three-handled quart cup that had belonged to her mother.

I was having a drink with Tapp one evening in the summer of 1912 and, as usual, reminiscing over Amy and her witchcraft when I decided it might be a good idea to camp out in the Green Walk that night. The weather was set fair, although with a slight tendency to thunder, and, who knows I thought, I might see the phantom wolf. Finishing my beer, I dashed off to see Tom Turner. He was quite pleased at the idea of sleeping under canvas for a few nights and together we collected our camping equipment, eventually settling down comfortably for the night with one side of the tent open. However, I could not sleep. It was very warm and close. Occasional flashes of lightning were visible in the distance. Silvery green and black patterns danced on the grass. Nearby an owl hooted mournfully.

Lying on my side and looking through the open tent flap I suddenly became aware of something moving along the Green Walk. My skin grew taut and a prickly feeling ran over my scalp. Thinking I must be dreaming I turned to look at Tom. He was awake also.

"Look, Tom," I gasped. "Look, along the path. Isn't that the phantom wolf?"

Tom laughed and said, "Good Lord! Surely you don't believe that nonsense." But as he looked in the direction in which I was pointing his eyes widened in fear. There, advancing slowly toward us and outlined in a luminous glow, was a huge wolf. Its jaws seemed to salivate with a phosphorescent drip. As it approached an evil smell filled the air. I began to recite the Lord's Prayer aloud: Tom hurriedly joined me. As we reached "deliver us from evil" there was a blinding flash of lightning, followed by a rumble of thunder. At the same time the wolf suddenly changed his course and made off along the Walk towards the cottage. As we watched another form emerged from the brambles near the wellhead. It appeared to be a grisly, greyish collie dog. There began a soundless but truly horrible fight between wolf and dog. Over the well, around the well, they snarled, rolled and jumped. Eventually the wolf seemed to lift the dog into the air and it disappeared into the well.

Horrorstruck we watched as the wolf, still outlined in a greenish glow, loped off towards the cottage and entered it through the closed door.

Another flash of lightning released us from our stunned, immobile state. We realized the cottage had been struck and already was blazing freely. The thatched roof and old timbers were very dry. Hurriedly pulling on our trousers we dashed off for help but in those days there was not even a telephone in the village. By the time the local fire brigade arrived the cottage had burned to the ground.

Some years later another cottage was built near the site of the old one. The well was cleaned out and rebuilt. During this renovation a curious three-handled quart cup, nearly filled with coins, was found in a niche in the side of the old well. And the skeleton of what appeared to be a collie dog was taken from the bottom of the well.

I have never found the courage to sleep again on the Green Walk – to find out if the wolf still runs there.

FATE September 1956

WEREWOLVES IN THAILAND
Ormond McGill

It was while visiting with Harold M. Young in Chiengmai, Thailand, that Ron Ormond and I first heard of the Taws. The Taws, it seems, are a form of mountain werewolf found among the Lahus, a tribe of mountain people living in the jungles bordering Northern Thailand and Burma. Here was a legend generally associated with Europe that also existed in the Orient, and obviously had some basis in truth.

Harold Young for years was an official of the Burmese government. During the period of British control, he was stationed among the remote tribes of the Shan and the Lahus. He finally left Burma due to political turmoil and he now lives in Chiengmai. A naturalist of note, he is the proprietor of the zoo in that city. Unquestionably he is one of the best-informed men in the world today on the Shan and Lahu peoples.

We were seated before a cheery fire in Young's spacious living room on the evening he told us this story. Filling his pipe, Harold looked out into space for a moment, lighted the pipe, and then slowly began:

"You say you are interested in searching out the mysterious and the unknown. I can tell you of things among the native people in these mountains that are uncanny; psychic phenomena that are daily occurrences. To me, it seems the more man retreats from nature behind the barrier of civilization, the farther he gets away from the basic powers which are the natural heritage of uncivilized man.

"Have you ever heard of the Taws?" he asked.

We shook our heads.

"The Taws," the naturalist went on, "are a form of native werewolf. Working among these natives, I had heard about them for years. They were described as strange, fearsome creatures with furry hides that at certain times of the month raid a village and either kill or carry off a victim.

"Native superstition I told myself; an excuse for carelessness in allowing a wild beast to get past the sentries and into the village. But that was before I had a personal experience of my own.

"About six months ago, I was on a hunting trip that took me to a Lahu village high in those mountains to the north that lie just on the Thai-Burma border." Harold pointed out of his window. "It had been quite a hike, but I love the mountain trails and was anxious to get in some night shooting. The Lahu are great hunters. They have always been most friendly to me, but this night, the chief raised his hand in denial of my wish as he said in his own language, 'Taw in close to village; you can no hunt now!'

"I was about to voice my objection at being detained in no uncertain terms, when a shriek cut through the night. It came from behind us; from a thatched hut standing close to the jungle's edge. My band flew to my pistol and I dashed towards the source of the scream. The chief and other natives followed more slowly behind me. I knew them as brave men whom I had seen face a snarling tiger, yet they seemed strangely reluctant to help. I heard them muttering the word, 'Taw, Taw, Taw.'

"I slowed as I approached the hut from which the scream had come and became more cautious. On tiptoe, I advanced to the only window and peered inside. There was a bright moon that night and the inside of the hut, seen through the opening, while at first only a dusky smudge soon came into focus as my eyes became adjusted. I saw a sight

I shall never forget to my dying day; one that literally lifted the hairs on my head. Within that hut, chewing on the slashed neck of a now dying woman, was the most terrifying of creatures. It was both manlike and beastlike. Its body was covered with coarse hair and in its head was a ghastly gash of a mouth from which slavered, about the cruel fangs, droppings of spittle. Its eyes were small and red in the darkness.

"I took in all of this in the fleeting of a second; then my pistol was pumping lead into the creature. With a wild yell, it leaped and was gone into the night. I called to the natives who came gingerly forward. Together we searched for the creature amongst the trees which grew to the back of the hut near the edge of the village clearing. It was nowhere to be found. This was incredible as I am an expert marksman and to have missed my target at such pointblank range was out of the question! I was sure that I had not missed, yet the Taw (which the natives insisted it was) was gone!

"The female victim was quite beyond our help. I tossed a robe over the body. We continued our search into the jungle brush about the place, but there was nothing. Defeated we huddled by the fire the rest of the night. There was very little talk; each man strangely silent in his own world of thought.

"It was not until the next morning, with the coming of light, that we began a fresh search. A new clue was now discovered. A line of blood stains led from the hut into the surrounding thickets. The Lahu, those master hunters, tracked the stains as they circled the village, only to reenter at the opposite end.

"Once out of the bush, I myself could see the blood splotches clearly upon the ground. They led into another hut. We all dashed forward and drew aside the skin door covering. Inside, lying on the bed, was a native. He was dead, his eyes open and glazed. The trail of blood ended in a pool on the floor of the hut – from a bullet hole in his side just below the heart. I had not missed.

"But this is not the creature I saw ripping at the woman's throat last night, this is a man," I protested.

"The chief spat full in the dead face. 'Taw,' he said!"

Harold Young ceased speaking. In the ensuing silence, broken only by the crackle of the fire on the hearth, we looked at each other. Young asked quietly, "Would you like to hear of another Taw experience?"

We nodded uncertainly.

"This one is not a personal experience of my own, but was told me by one of my beloved Shan friends in the mountains of Burma. There were two young men – hunters who habitually made their excursions on foot down a path leading into the jungle that took them by one of the Burial Caves of the Dead. These people, as you may know, bury their recent dead in caves with the corpse sitting upright. Each day in passing, one young man told his friend to proceed on that he might in loneliness pay his homage to the dead within. Understanding the whim, his friend would comply, to be rejoined a bit later by the other man.

"This procedure continued. Eventually the suspicions of the second young man became aroused. While pretending to pass on down the path, he doubled back and saw his friend disappearing within the burial cave. Cautiously he stole forward. Inside the cave be saw a creature, hairy and horrible, or so it seemed to him in the dim light.

It was hunched over a dead corpse calmly munching the remains.

"Instinctively, he drew his crossbow and fired the arrow through the creature's skull. It toppled forward across the corpse. With his foot, he turned it over. The eyes which met his were the eyes of his friend. Then as they closed in death and as he continued to gaze in horror the entire visage metamorphosed, from those of a beast to the handsome features of the young man he had known.

"'Taw,' he screamed, as he turned and ran from the cave."

"Is it true, Harold?" we asked incredulously.

"It is true, the mountain people do not lie about such things," he answered.

Ormond McGill: Naturalist and author.

FATE June 1961

THE WOLFMAN OF AVELOSO
J.M. Andrade

It was an ordinary day in the small village of Aveloso, near Meda in northern Portugal. Farmers already had begun their day's work and housewives had gone shopping. In the village school, a small, one classroom building, the elderly schoolteacher had just started the day's lesson. On this, just another school day, nothing seemed in any way out of the ordinary.

Then suddenly eight-year-old Albano started screaming and shrieking. His face took on a wild expression, his fingers twitched and he fell on all fours, jumping to and fro as he wrecked the desks in the classroom. The terrified teacher fled, followed by the near-hysterical children. Some strong men tried to subdue the little boy but his quick jumps and amazing strength made that impossible. Eventually the fit ended. When it did, Albano could not remember what he had done; he could only say, "I've been sleeping."

Albano de Jesus was born at Aveloso in 1880. His parents were peasants and his father died when he was a baby. Neither parent had a history of mental illness, and for his first few years he seemed an ordinary, lively boy. When he was seven, his mother sent him to the village school and a year later the fits began.

As the fits came back again and again during the next few weeks, Albano's mother finally took him to a doctor and to as many "healers" as she heard about. But no one could tell what was wrong with him, let alone cure him. In any case, Albaninho (little Albano), as he was known, was harmless enough if let alone and between fits he was as normal as any boy. Soon the village got used to him. Old women, claiming he had been bewitched, called him "Albano of the Evil" behind his back but nobody abused or mistreated him.

As he grew, stories of his exploits spread throughout the country. He was almost a superman during his fits. He could jump up to 30 feet into the air and also from tree to tree, a feat that caused local journalists to call him the "ape-man." He seemed to defy gravity. He could walk on fire without being burned or run about in the snow, often naked, without being frostbitten. He could drink enormous amounts of liquids – any liquids – with no unpleasant consequences. And after the fits were over, he had not a single scratch or ache.

One day in August 1904 Albaninho's cousin, a policeman in Lisbon, Portugal's capital city, came to Aveloso to visit his family and agreed to take Albaninho, already 24 years old, to see his older sister who also lived in Lisbon. The journey by train was uneventful enough, as was Albaninho's first night at his sister's.

The next morning, however, he had three successive fits, running away from home, chasing passing tramcars and jumping onto their roofs. He clung to power cables and rolled up and down the streets. Two squads of policemen tried to capture him but he reacted so violently that they limited themselves to clearing the area of passersby and waiting. Eventually the officers took Albaninho to the city jail, where he spent the night and the following day without causing any trouble. But on the third day, after he had had a violent fit in his cell, a psychiatrist conducted a cursory examination and announced that Albaninho was suffering from an acute form of lycanthropy – the disease of werewolves.

No definitive explanation has yet been found for lycanthropy, although it was first studied in depth by the Roman physician Marcellus, a contemporary of Emperor Hadrian. Several cases are reported by Pliny, Petronius, Virgil and other ancient writers. The poet Ovid relates that

Albano de Jesus, left, suffered from lycanthropy, the rare werewolf disease
which has been known since Roman times.

Jupiter punished the Arcadian tyrant Lycaon ("wolf like") by turning him
into a werewolf. The mythological satyrs had werewolf characteristics.
The disease brought upon Nebuchadnezzar by the Lord as related in the
Bible (Daniel 4:32-33) may have been lycanthropy.

So Albaninho was sent to a local mental hospital, given electric
shocks for a time with no results and not long afterwards released and
sent back to his village. Back in Aveloso, Albaninho's notoriety grew.
During his fits, he would run toward the local cemetery, jump over its
wall, walk and jump on the graves, and finally break into the storage
hut, where he usually would squat in an empty coffin. Press accounts
describe similar behavior during his short stay in Lisbon. His antics

there attracted huge crowds. But in his home village such behavior was so commonplace that nobody thought much about it.

For some reason Albaninho showed a deep hatred of dogs during his fits. If he came across one he would literally rip it apart. Once he killed wolves with his bare hands. On market days, he sometimes attacked horses or oxen, occasionally causing stampedes and appreciable damage to market stalls but never injuring himself. If a locked door attracted his attention, he would sometimes break it open with his fists, feet and head. But he seldom turned on people and when he did his victims were individuals who had been cruel to him. But he did not really hurt even these.

One day, during a fit, he charged a small house which was under construction, scared the workers away and brought down its half-finished walls with kicks and pushes. In the process, he was partly buried under the debris. The workers prudently waited for some time, then lifted up the heavy stones (northern Portugal's traditional building material) to free what they assumed would be Albaninho's dead body. But they were startled to discover he was alive and uninjured: he was also back to his normal self. He simply stood up and walked away as if nothing had happened.

This was too much for the village. At the local people's request, he was deported to the West African colony of Angola, where Portugal frequently sent its social misfits. On the way to Africa he had several fits aboard the ship. He would jump overboard and then jump off the water back onto the ship, although in his normal state he could not swim. He stayed in Luanda, Angola's main city, for some time during the 1920s but the disturbances continued. Finally, he was arrested and taken to the Fortress, a 16th-century building used as a jail. In the course of yet another fit he bent his cell window's bars, squeezed between them and dove into the sea. The authorities decided they had no legal basis for detaining him any longer, so they sent him back home. His village would have to learn to live with him.

As a young man, although he was sociable enough between fits, Albaninho was never invited to dances or parties because his fits, which erupted without warning, frightened the girls. His peculiar condition rendered him officially unfit for work: he never learned a trade and lived on a pension given him by Queen Amelia of Portugal and on gifts from friends and visiting scientists.

Years later a local divorcee fell in love with him and bore him two daughters, both normal: but after seven years she suddenly grew afraid of him and left home, never to return. His daughters never reached adulthood. One died in infancy, the other in her late teens.

Albaninho's fits disappeared forever when he was 43. No one knew why. Albaninho's explanation was that Our Lady of Remedies had cured him. During a period of a few weeks between fits, he said, he had asked the Virgin to work a miracle and promised her a high mass of thanksgiving. She responded by relieving him of his terrible affliction.

Albaninho had always been a Christian although he had been banned from church services as a child for obvious reasons. Consequently, he never bothered too much about religion. But in his last years parish priest Father Lacerda tried to bring him back into the Church and eventually succeeded in hearing him in confession.

In 1976, when Albaninho was 96, he had a premonition that he had little time to live. He suddenly remembered that he had never paid the promise he made to the Virgin. Although suffering from acute thrombosis in both legs – he had been in the hospital because of it more than once – he insisted that two friends carry him from village to village and help him collect money for the thanksgiving mass. Father Lacerda finally set a date for its celebration but it was already too late.

Gangrene set in both Albaninho's legs and his condition became so serious that Father Lacerda had him sent to the nearest hospital, in Guarda, despite Albaninho's requests to be allowed to die in his own village. On the day following his admission to the hospital, he had a stroke and never regained consciousness. He died on August 4, 1976.

After a hurried postmortem, his body was enclosed in a lead coffin, which was sealed and taken to Aveloso for burial.

But Albaninho was fated to be controversial even in death. As the coffin was being carried to the village church, it burst and a foul-smelling liquid flowed freely through a crack. The body had apparently decomposed within some 24 hours of death. The stench was so overwhelming that the church ceremony was canceled and the coffin hastily buried. Two days later the smell inside the church was still unbearable. The building had to be disinfected and perfumed before it once again was suitable for normal services.

Thus ended the unhappy life of Albano de Jesus, the wolfman of Aveloso, the victim of a condition no one ever understood, least of all himself. Yet, although it left him a branded man for the rest of his life, he tried to live with it as best he could. Perhaps the best proof that he succeeded is in the words of the villagers who tell the researchers who occasionally visit Aveloso: "He was a good man. May God grant him eternal rest."

FATE September 1980

SAVED BY A SILVER BULLET
Leo Heiman

Werewolves and vampires went out of fashion in the Balkans during the Second World War. Four years of German occupation followed by two decades of communist rule were not conducive to superstitious and supernatural horror tales, for compared to sojourns in Gestapo interrogation rooms and arrest by Communist secret police a visit from Count Dracula and his cohorts was a mild nuisance.

Therefore I was surprised to learn that the inhabitants of Budva, a small village on Yugoslavia's Adriatic coast a few miles north of the Albanian border, one again was being terrorized by tales of a werewolf who was said to control a few square miles of territory between the mountains and the sea. My first reaction on hearing this 1966 version of the old legend was that it must be a publicity gimmick designed to attract sensation-hungry tourists, or life under Yugoslavia's relaxed brand of "national Communism" had become so good and carefree that people once again had time to worry about Dracula and Company.

I first heard of Budva's werewolf when I rented a house on a narrow promontory leading from the village to the crumbling ruins of an old castle built by the Turks in the 17th century and designed to control the pirate-infested waters between Albania and the offshore Adriatic islands. Yugoslavia's official policy of attracting tourists to stay for longer periods and spend more money made it cheaper for me to rent a house with a cook and gardener-servant for two weeks than to stay one week in a first-rate hotel. I had a lot of writing to do. Hotel guests usually protested the clatter of my typewriter late at night and after inspecting the house and its spacious verandah overlooking the placid sea I immediately moved in.

The narrow dusty track leading from the village to the old Turkish castle was hemmed in by the sea on one side and sheer cliffs on the other. Apart from a few clapboard shacks used by the local fishermen in the daytime there were few other buildings on the promontory. Directly opposite my house was the entrance to a cave, partially covered by dense vegetation and foliage. To the right of the house a curious structure loomed over the deserted beach. A huge stone wheel with a circular aperture in the center was cemented sidewise onto a broad base of stone blocks similar to those used in the walls of the Turkish fortress.

When I asked old Katisa, the cook who came with the house, the purpose of the stone wheel she mumbled something, crossed herself and knelt to pray, ignoring the odor of burning onions from the frying pan on the kitchen range.

Simeon the gardener was more cooperative. After looking furtively around he too crossed himself, then led me to the wheel and pointing to some reddish stains on some of the stones said, "When the Turks executed prisoners or tortured local inhabitants who resisted their oppressive rule they led their victims to this stone, inserted their hands and feet through the hole, one by one, chopped them off with an axe and left them to bleed to death. The whole beach here is soaked with the blood of Christian martyrs and this naturally has attracted all kinds of unsavory elements. The cave you see across the road was the home of a werewolf. As long as he could lap up Christian blood freely he did not attack people. But when the Turks were driven out and the executions stopped the werewolf began snatching children and dragging them to his lair to drink their blood. And now they say he is back again..." He paused and crossed himself twice.

"Who says?" I persisted.

"The people who saw him."

After a few shots of pungent Slivovits plum brandy, reinforced by a pack of American cigarettes, Simeon told me the rest of the werewolf story.

The man who allegedly sold his soul to the devil and signed a pact with the forces of hell was Count Erasmus Von Windyschatz, an Austrian nobleman who fought the Turks in the 17th century. After quarreling with his commanding general in the Battle of Turnovo in 1678 he defected to the Turks, embraced the Moslem faith and ultimately was appointed commandant of the Budva fortress and chief executioner of Christian prisoners. Like all renegades Count Erasmus exceeded his masters in cruelty and zeal. Whenever any of his old comrades from the Agram Regiment were captured and brought to be tortured on the stone wheel he personally chopped off their limbs and then drank victory toasts from the cups made of human skulls and filled with their blood mixed with wine. A sadist to begin with, he ultimately went insane and began attacking local people without provocation. Fearing major disorders the Turkish government deposed him from the fortress commandant's post. So Count Erasmus went underground, hiding in the cave from which he emerged at night to raid farm houses and fishing huts. Like most legends in this part of the world the Count Erasmus probably was built on solid historical facts and subsequently embellished with grisly details added by each successive generation.

But why bring the unsavory Count Erasmus back to life in 1966? Simeon the gardener had no logical explanation. But he pointed out that what looked to me like a bargain – a five-room house with all modern comforts, two servants and free food for $8.00 a day – was in fact no bargain at all. The house was offered cheap by the local tourist office because no one could live in it for more than one or two nights. The werewolf always scared them away.

When I laughed aloud Simeon again made the sign of the cross, drained the bottle of Slivovits in one gulp and told me the house had been empty for several years. The previous inhabitant had been a Chief Pilot of JAT, the Yugoslav Air Lines, who had rented it as a summer retreat for his honeymoon. He had stayed with his young wife in the house for one week in June, 1963 – until the werewolf came.

The pilot had been out in the bay fishing from a rowboat by the light of kerosene lanterns at dusk and his wife had been preparing dinner on the open verandah. He suddenly heard her screaming in anguish and horror. Looking across the 300 yards of water, he had seen a dark shape, its head surround by a phosphorescent green aura, looming behind her. She had struggled feebly and then gone limp in the apparition's arms. Her husband saw her dragged back to a dark corner of the verandah. He had shouted for help as he rowed at top speed towards the beach. An oar broke and he had jumped into the water to swim ashore. When he stormed up the stairs brandishing a sharp stone his wife had showed no signs of life. She was bleeding profusely from two jagged wounds in her throat and her face was scratched as if by an animal's claws.

An ambulance had rushed the unconscious woman and her frantic husband to a nearby Yugoslav naval base where surgeons at a military hospital had saved her life with blood transfusions and immediate surgery on her injured neck. But her mind became permanently unhinged. She could give no coherent account of who or what attacked her on the verandah.

Police investigation produced no results. There were no fingerprints or clues except for a few spots of caked mud which smelled of sulphur. Bloodhounds led the officers across the road to the cave entrance where they halted, whined fearfully and refused to enter.

A police search party, led by veteran cave explorers, was organized to probe the dark recesses of the cave, hunting for man or animal. The men proceeded for about 30 yards along a narrow tunnel which also smelled of sulphur until they found further progress barred by huge slabs of granite which could not be budged. Assuming that a rogue bear used the cave as his hideout and had emerged from it to attack the woman, police sent engineers to black the cave's entrance with sandbags and concrete and likewise closed their file.

The case of the pilot's wife was hushed up by the authorities who feared that publicity would ruin the tourist trade along this part of the Adriatic coast. But the people of Budva knew better than to accept the official explanation. As far as they were concerned Count Erasmus Von Windyschatz had come back from hell to gorge on Christian blood. And when they found the official sandbags and concrete removed and the cave entrance again open they began to give the place a wide berth and to lock themselves in their houses at night.

There were further unexplained assaults on young women including the most recent one in May, 1966. Seventeen-year-old Jelka Dubasevic had returned home from the Communist Youth Club and suddenly remembered having left her rubber boots in her father's fishing shack on the promontory where she had been helping him sort out the catch earlier that day. Turning back she was passing between the stone wheel and the cave entrance when a dark shape leaped at her out of the shadows and sank its teeth in the nape of her neck. Jelka screamed and fainted. Local fishermen, alerted by her scream, had arrived to rescue her just in time. Surgeons at the hospital, examining the wounds, said the incisions were made by the teeth of a mad dog or wolf. They cured her completely in 10 days.

The villagers now took things into their own hands. They contacted friends in a marble quarry near Titograd and obtained dynamite sticks and blasting caps. They put them into the cave, lit the fuse and retreated to a safe distance. Reportedly the blast was terrific; clouds of dust and smoke belched out of the cave's mouth and a landslide partially covered the opening.

But apparently nothing could hurt the werewolf. Numerous persons had sworn they had seen the ghostly apparition on several occasions after the blast.

"Who owns this house?" I asked Simeon.

"The community of Budva."

"I know; I rented it from them. But it must have been built before the war. Who was the original owner?"

It transpired that the house was much older than I had thought. It was built before the First World War by an officer of the Imperial Austrian-Hungarian navy. At the time Austria controlled the entire Adriatic coast and operated a major naval base on nearby Kotor (Cataro) Bay. Between the two world wars the house was leased to a Yugoslav engineer from Zagreb who used it as a summer retreat for his family. When the Germans occupied Yugoslavia he became a turncoat and joined the pro-Nazi Ustasha Corps which perpetrated war crimes and brutalities on a part with Nazi storm troops and Gestapo goon squads. He returned to Budva to punish the local people, most of whom supported Marsha Tito's Communist Partisans. In retaliation the guerillas tossed a homemade bomb into his bedroom killing his wife and daughter. But the traitor had been shielded from the blast by his wife's body and had escaped with minor injuries. He was sentenced to death in absentia by a Partisan Tribunal but the sentence was never carried out because he could not be found after the war.

Following the liberation of Budva by Tito's Partisans in September, 1944, the house was seized by the People's Council and is now joint community property. No one wanted to live in it and the councilors had handed it over to the tourist office to be rented for a nominal fee. I was the first tenant to move in – in 1966.

Katisa prepared dinner, served it and after she had washed the dishes lit out for home, crossing herself as she passed the stone wheel and the mouth of the cave. Simeon made sure all the lights worked and the locks closed properly and then asked permission to go home too. But after 20 minutes he came back riding a bicycle and carrying an old single-barreled, muzzle-loading shotgun.

"I have loaded it with a silver bullet, sir," he said placing the weapon near my typewriter on the table.

"What for?" I asked.

"In case the werewolf attacks you – the only thing that can hurt him is a silver bullet. He fears neither steel nor fire and ordinary bullets do not hurt him, either."

I did not wish to appear ungrateful. After all Simeon had showed devotion and courage by returning after dusk. I stood on the front porch until he disappeared around the bend, pedaling furiously as if participating in the Tour De France. Then I went in and locked the doors.

I placed my typewriter on the verandah's heavy wooden table facing the sea and with two fingers typed out the rough draft of an article analyzing the recent political upheavals in Yugoslavia. The transistor radio played at my elbow full blast the latest pop tunes on Belgrade's Hit Parade and I took an occasional swig from the brandy bottle as I worked well past midnight. Simeon's shotgun with the silver bullet leaned against the wall behind my back where I had placed it. This probably saved my life.

The kerosene lanterns of sardine fishermen flickered off the coast and the soft breeze wafted smells of charcoal-grilled steaks from the barbecue pits of Jadranski Hotel on the other side of the village. I don't know just when I became aware of another smell. But suddenly it penetrated my senses that the pungent smell of sulphur was getting stronger every second. I pinched myself to make sure that I was not dreaming and gulped a swallow of the fiery liquid to kill the stench. I told myself that my mind must be reacting to the horror tales I had heard and was now fabricating the illusory smell of sulphur.

Suddenly a lopsided shadow flickered against the brighter background of the moonlit sea, moving across the verandah with incredible speed. Even now I cannot say whether it was man or animal. But the smell of sulphur was overwhelming and the wooden table was bathed in a greenish glow.

An involuntary cry escaped from my throat as I kicked at the table and rolled backwards with my chair, reaching for Simeon's shotgun. I am a veteran of two wars and I probably was saved by my trained instantaneous reaction. The heavy gun fell on top of me as I rolled to the left to escape the bear-like shape which leaped at my throat. My fingers groped for the trigger. There was no time to take aim. I just swiveled the heavy barrel into the crook of my arm and fired.

My eardrums were almost split by the blast. The gun's recoil brought the solid metal-encased butt hammering against my ribs with the force of a baseball bat. I was pinned to the floor and could not move as a bright tongue of flame belched out of the muzzle. I do not know whether the silver bullet hit my attacker at all. But the smell of sulphur receded and all that remained in the way of direct evidence of the encounter was a gaping hole in a sturdy plank which supported the verandah railings.

No one in the village heard the shot. No one came and I spent a sleepless night waiting for Simeon's return in the morning.

He took one look at my face and crossed himself. Together we searched for further evidence. The garden was walled and the attacker must have entered the sea and waded across 20 yards of shallow water to approach the house from the rear. We found no footprints on the rocky ground beneath the waterline and the verandah. But two railings were splintered where the "apparition" had hurled itself at them in a rush to escape. We discovered no blood spots or shreds of fabric but the railings still smelled faintly of sulphur.

With the sharp point of a hunting knife Simeon dug out the silver bullet from the plank. He handed it to me. "Wear it on your neck from a silver chain as a good luck charm," he suggested.

I gave it back to him. "I am moving out today, Simeon, and you can use it again. This old cannon of yours really works fine."

He grinned under his bushy moustache, "So, you believe me now, don't you, sir?"

I shrugged. "There is nothing supernatural about it but it's a mystery all right. I never heard of bears or wolves entering houses to attack human beings but animals too suffer from deranged minds. It could be a rogue bear with a grudge against mankind who lives in the cave and regards anyone in the house across the road as his personal enemy – or a mad wolf, or a lunatic. Perhaps the Yugoslav traitor who was blasted out of this house by the Partisans went mad, hides in the cave and emerges to attack anyone who occupies his property. There must be mineral springs deep in the cave, hence the smell of sulphur. And there is no lack of food either. The villagers lock themselves in their houses at night and anyone can approach their fields, orchards, gardens and chicken coops. Everything can be rationalized but I am moving out…"

Simeon advised against informing the police. "Cops are the same all over, sir. First, they will assume you were drunk. Then they will think you are crazy. Even if they believe you they will try to hush it up for fear of ruining the tourist trade. They know from experience that such investigations do not pay off and they can expect only reprimands, no promotions, from their superiors. If you persist they will ask you to stay in Budva until the investigation is completed. This may take weeks or even months. I am sure you do not want that, do you?"

I was in complete agreement with the gardener. I told him to divide the two weeks' supply of food with Katisa and gave them $50 each before driving north to Titograd and Belgrade.

***

There is a sequel to this werewolf story – two postscripts, in fact.

In Belgrade, I went to see Commissioner Zvonko Petrovac, the official in charge of war crimes files at the Ministry of State Security. He listened to my request for information about the trial of Peter Bkarski, the traitor from Budva, and pushed a button on his desk. A secretary brought in the dusty folders a few minutes later.

"Bkarski? He was apprehended by the People's Militia in 1948 and imprisoned in Zagreb Penitentiary. His death sentence was reviewed by a special court and commuted to life imprisonment. But in 1963 he benefitted from the sweeping amnesty promulgated by the government on occasion of President Tito's 70th birthday. He was released and his present whereabouts are unknown although he was supposed to report to the police in his new place of residence…."

The werewolf of Budva made his reappearance in the summer of 1963 – after the amnesty!

Dr. Ivan Macric, of the Mineral Prospecting Department at the Ministry of Mines, informed me that plans are underway to tap mineral springs along the Adriatic shore for health resorts and chemical exploitation.

"What about the cave at Budva?" I wanted to know. It contains sulphur springs and phosphorus deposits."

He looked at me curiously. "How do you know?"

"From personal experience," I said. And I described my meeting with the werewolf.

He unfolded a large map of the coastal sector on his desk and drew a fat red circle around the Budva promontory. This means 'For Immediate Prospecting.' Whoever hides inside, we'll smoke him out!"

But will they? Can they?

Leo Heiman: Polish journalist, foreign correspondent, and author, and editor of a syndicated Israeli newspaper.

FATE December 1967

THE HOME OF THE LOUP-GAROU
James T. Farley

Z ombies can be rationalized. At least a semi-logical explanation can be offered on behalf of these so-called "living dead." But the *loup-garou,* the werewolf of Haiti, poses a problem. I can only detail my experiences; interpretation lies in hypothesis.

Haiti, in February 1944, was not the tourist stop it is today. In Cap Haiten, tucked away in the rugged northeast corner of this Negro republic, the *citoyen* went stoically about their business. To them the war existed, certainly, but *pas ici,* not here. The Autobahn was the road to Berlin but in Cap Haiten the Au de Cap Road led to market.

I first learned of the werewolf when I rented a house in the Bel Air section of the Cape. Here, astride the road leading to the ruins of the huge castle built by Napoleon for his sister, houses were scarce. The narrow, dusty road, bounded by the ocean on one side and a sheer cliff on the other, boasted few habitants.

From my verandah, the restless sea glimmered through the vivid foliage of a flamboyant tree. To the left twined a lush tangle of jungle; at the rear of the house loomed the cliff. Twenty yards to my right crouched the house of the *loup-garou*.

It seemed a rather small house, only one story high. A breadfruit tree spread protecting branches over its slanting roof. The uncurtained windows peered, like sightless eyes, over a crumbling stone wall in the front of which was set a wrought iron gate.

The few Haitians who passed did so with quickened pace and lowered heads. And each soul made the sign of the cross as he came abreast of the gate.

Knowing the Haitian penchant for employing this sign as a talisman against evil spirits, I determined to learn the reason for this.

My sources of information, as always in such matters, was my chauffeur, Fetius Jean. Together we had tracked the elusive zombie and I had come to rely on his courage and cool judgment. In response to this question, however, Fetius started nervously and, glancing in the direction of the house, crossed himself. Then, but by unwilling bit, the legend of the *loup-garou* unfolded.

The house, explained Fetius, had been empty for several years. The owner was an officer in the Garde de Haiti and, consequently, a person of some social standing. To the peasants, however, he was known as a *loup-garou*, a wolf man.

Now, the *loup-garou* is comparatively rare in Haiti. It is nocturnal, venturing abroad only when the moon has reached its zenith. Bathed in a phosphorescent green cloud, it is capable of covering vast distances. Vampirical, it feeds on human blood, preferably the blood of children.

The apparition, Fetius continued, had been observed frequently in the house and about the ground during the time of M_____'s residence.

Fanned by fear, the flames of fear had begun their dance to the pulsing throb of the *Rada* drums as the peasant plotted the destruction of their nemesis. Aware of the temper of these fierce northerners, the hard core of many revolutions, Colonel _____, the commanding officer, had prudently transferred M _____ to the garrison at Port au Prince. Thus ostensibly, the menace was removed and indolence regained possession of the streets.

Until the return of the loup-garou!

A young Haitian couple with a year-old child leased the house and promptly moved in. Strangers to Cap Haitien, they had made the long journey from Aux Cayes in the south. A *camion* unloaded their belongings and they spent the first day getting settled in their new home. That night, with the child asleep in his crib, they retired early, fatigued by their efforts.

Sometime during the night they were roused by the shrill screams of the child. Rushing to the crib they found it empty! The child was gone!

Frantic with fear they searched and found the baby on the floor, just outside the doorway, apparently dropped there by its molester during a hasty flight. It was uninjured except for two shallow punctures in the throat which bled sparingly. As they laid the child back in its crib they became aware of a rapidly receding greenish glow and smelled the faint but pungent odor of brimstone.

Now recognizing the nature of the marauder, they huddled, terror stricken, through the balance of the seemingly endless night. At dawn the man went into town and engaged a *camion*. By the time the sun streamed in the windows the house was, again, empty. So it had remained empty these past few years.

Often at night, said Fetius, the eerie green glow was seen floating past the windows and flickering through the yard, fleetingly visible behind the masking wall.

Fetius pleaded with me to abandon my new quarters. He feared the *loup-garou* would seek to harm me as a transgressor. In reply, I suggested that he spend a few nights at the house with me and together we would stalk my ghostly neighbor. Shaking his head, he backed away and, surprised by his obvious terror, I dismissed him for the day.

Davius, my houseboy, prepared dinner and after he had washed the dishes I sent him home; his relief was quite apparent.

Closing the large wooden door, I dropped the heavy latch bar into place. After extinguishing the light, I retired to my bedroom which was separated from the main room by a louvred door. Closing the door behind me I undressed rapidly, climbed through the mosquito netting and fell into bed. Sleep came willingly and immediately.

Sometime later I awoke abruptly and sat bolt upright in the bed; a sound had penetrated my sleeping senses. As I sat there, in groggy confusion, the sound came again.

Something was pushing against the iron door!

I distinctly heard the rattle of the latch bar as the door yielded. Throwing aside the netting, I leaped to the floor, fumbling frantically for the loaded .45 on the night table. My fingers closed on the comforting feel of the cold metal, and, releasing the safety, I reached quietly for the handle of the connecting door.

Suddenly the light in the other room blazed into brilliance. Certain the intruder had gained the house I threw open the door and rushed into the room.

It was empty!

The naked bulb swung forward and back causing the shadows to writhe and twist in frenzied abandon. The latch bar was still in place, seemingly undisturbed. Removing it, I opened the massive door and stepped onto the verandah.

In the faint light of the crescent moon the branches of the flamboyant tree gestured warningly of the perils abroad in the night. But the darkness was still, no rustle of furtive movement intruded upon its serenity.

Turning to re-enter the house, I was startled to see a light hovering in the window of the empty building beyond the wall. My first impression was of a flashlight in the hands of someone moving about within the house. Then my hackles rose as I saw that the light was diffused rather than direct and was green in color. Simultaneously I became aware of an unpleasant bite in my nostrils. *It was, unmistakably, brimstone!*

Panic seized me and I rushed back into the house and hastily barred the door. Until dawn I sat in the harsh light of the stark bulb with the .45 cocked and ready in my hand.

When Davius arrived at 7:00 A.M. I refrained from mentioning the weird happenings of the night. No did I inform Fetius Jean when he arrived with the car. I met his inquiring glance with a smile and a sham aura of confidence. Truthfully, I was still very much shaken, but I was determined to seek an early answer in the mystery.

That same afternoon, on my way home from the sisal fields, I stopped at the house of Dr. _____, the Anglican missionary. The good man had gone to Bayeux for a few days but his daughter and her two stalwart brothers were at home. I invited them to dine with me promising some excitement in lieu of dessert, and they accepted with alacrity.

My incomparable Davius surpassed himself in their honor and we dined exceedingly well.

Following his departure, I detailed the events of the previous night to Audrey, David and George. Familiar with the legend of the *loup-garou*, their excitement mounted as I disclosed my plan. An unexpected visit by Raphael and his sister Estelle added reinforcements, and they enthusiastically joined our ranks.

We decided to extinguish the light and sit quietly on the verandah to await the appearance of the *loup-garou*. Darkness fell, the trade winds blew caressingly from the sea and, as always, subsided suddenly. The moon began its ascent of the heavens. The only sound was the faint groan of the branches of the flamboyant tree. We conversed in subdued whispers, all eyes straining intently toward the house of the *loup-garou*.

David caught the first dim flicker and his sibilant hiss warned the others. Then we all saw the undulating green glow as it passed first one window and then another of the presumably empty house.

It had been agreed that, together with the boys, I would investigate the house while the girls watched from the safety of the verandah. David and George were armed with stout canes, Raphael brandished a machete and I carried the bulky .45. Silently we moved off the verandah as the girls huddled together in mutual support.

In accordance with our pre-arranged plan, Raphael posted himself to the rear of the house, David and George scaled the walls at either side, and I entered through the front gate. Certain that our prey would prove to be nothing more than a vagrant, I expected that, flushed from cover, he would break for the main entrance.

The gate squealed in rust protest and abruptly a light stopped at a front window and as quickly vanished.

"Now," I shouted and leaped for the front steps. The door was unlocked and I plunged through as the boys hurtled through the windows.

The room was empty! The light had disappeared!

All that remained of our quarry was a faint sulphuric tang of brimstone. Meticulously we searched each of the three small rooms. Layers of dust, undisturbed by footprints, covered the floors. Rejoining us, Raphael swore that no one had left the house by the rear either before or during the assault.

Before leaving, each of us verified the odor in the house and identified it as brimstone.

David and George stated that they too had observed the light before leaping down the walls. Back on the verandah, the girls confirmed Raphael's report.

No one had left the house.

We settled down to await a possible reappearance of the spectre. *And we were not disappointed!*

Three times in the next two hours the light appeared and each appearance was followed by our stealthy attack.

We saw nothing, the dust remained undisturbed except for our footprints. Each time, however, we noted the by now familiar scent of the *loup-garou.*

Finally, at midnight, we gave up the chase and, swearing each other to confidence, we said goodnight and parted.

Retiring, I slept soundly and if I was visited during the night I was not disturbed.

For the two months, I remained neighbor to the *loup-garou.* I saw the light on numerous occasions. Always I wondered; often I was afraid. I made no further attempts to investigate the phenomenon. I deemed it safer to accept the evidence of the poltergeist without substantiation. And my decision to move away was prompted by the repetitious events which occurred several nights each week. The rattle of the door latch, the unpredictable behavior of the light in the living room, loud thumpings on the roof and the walls of my house all combined to fill me with nervous tension. Even more frightening was the constant odor of brimstone. I began to fear for my personal safety and well-being. Certain that, rationalize as I might, the thing was after me. I allowed discretion to overcome valor and retired from the field.

On a rainy April morning, as Fetius waited nervously in the car, I took a last long look at my mysterious neighbor and departed.

As we drove past the gate of the house of the *loup-garou,* unconsciously I joined Fetius in a swift gesture.

I crossed myself.

James T. Farley: Professional writer sent to Haiti during World War II to work on rubber and sisal development.

FATE October 1963

DOGMEN
AND
THE BEAST OF BRAY ROAD

MICHIGAN DOG MAN SIGHTING
Simon A. Thalmann

It was a rainy, foggy summer night when a Portage, Michigan, woman drove home around 10 p.m. She came upon something that looked like a creature lying in the middle of the road on Highland Drive. Kathryn, 52, who asked that her last name be kept private, said at first, she thought the creature was a person. Then she noticed the brownish hair covering its entire body as it stood and ran off in the glare of her headlights on its hind legs.

Eerily human
"I was so scared," she said. "Normally I would've backed my car and shone the lights in the woods ... but I mean, it flipped me out. I was scared to death so I just kept going."

Kathryn, who has lived in the area for 32 years and never had such an experience before, said the creature was thin and about five feet tall. It had a strange, lumbering gait and an eerily human face. "It looked like somebody that was dressed up in a costume or something," she said. "It was a freaky looking thing."

Kathryn was so distraught when she arrived home that she called the Portage police to report the incident. The police said they would send someone out to check the area.

"I still felt at that time that it was a person," Kathryn said, adding that she questioned why anyone would be out in such a secluded area at night and in such bad weather. She can see the area where the creature appeared from the front door of her house, and although she watched for the police for a long time, she said she doesn't believe they ever came.

When Kathryn told her family what she had seen, they were hesitant to believe her. Some laughed.

The Beast of Bray Road by Linda S. Godfrey. Used with permission.

Linda S. Godfrey is used to hearing reports of similar sightings. A former journalist, Godfrey broke the story concerning a rash of sightings of a mysterious, werewolf-like creature in the woods surrounding Bray Road in Elkhorn, Wisconsin. The books that resulted from her research, *The Beast of Bray Road: Tailing Wisconsin's Werewolf*, and *Hunting the American Werewolf*, became the basis for the *"American Werewolf"* episode of *Monster Quest* on the History Channel. Ever since, she has been considered an expert on mysterious, bipedal, canine-like creatures.

An October article in the *Kalamazoo Gazette*, in which Godfrey was interviewed, led Kathryn to come forward with her story.

Intelligent wolf?

The *Gazette* had interviewed Godfrey concerning a creature known in Michigan as the Dog Man, a large, canine like, bipedal creature residents across the state have reportedly seen for decades, if not longer.

Although Kathryn doesn't claim to know whether it was the Dog Man she saw that night, her experience is similar to sightings of the creature Godfrey has received. The sightings came not only from Michigan, but from all over the country, and sometimes from those outside the U.S. as well.

"I've talked to hundreds of people who've seen it and they're all quite convinced they saw something real," Godfrey said. "I haven't seen it myself, but I believe that there's something that all these people are seeing. I don't think they're all crazy or anything like that."

Godfrey thinks the Dog Man could be a large species of wolf that has adapted over time to walk upright, an adaptation that also could have led to an increase in intelligence to the extent that the creature could keep itself hidden. "In general, freeing your forelimbs for other purposes will build up parts of the brain that wouldn't be activated otherwise. And they say that is one factor that made humans smarter, so why wouldn't that make canines smarter too?"

Godfrey thinks the creature could possibly be a being from another dimension or the spirit world. "Really, the door is open, and I refuse to put a label on it because once you decide it's one thing, you close the door on investigations; you may as well just quit."

Though the nature of the Dog Man is uncertain, Godfrey is convinced that something exists that people are seeing. "If it's not real, there's some really strange mass hallucination that's unexplainable by science, probably more unexplainable by science than a canine that manages to adapt itself to walk upright sometimes."

Officials uncertain

Although Kalamazoo is listed by Godfrey as an area in Michigan of multiple reported sightings of the Dog Man, officials in the Kalamazoo area said they have never received a single report matching Godfrey's description. Many had never even heard of the Dog Man.

Diane Malv, records clerk at the Portage police department, said there's no report under Kathryn's name on file with the department. She said reports of animals of a suspicious nature are sent to the Department of Natural Resources. The Kalamazoo sheriff's department said they would either pass such a report on to the DNR or to animal control.

Sara Schaefer, southwest Michigan supervisor of the wildlife division for the DNR, said they get reports of suspicious sightings but there is never any evidence for them to investigate the claims. "If it's just a sighting there's nothing to do, because no matter what it is, it's gone by the time we get there. If there's evidence, like they have tracks that are still there or hair or something like that, then we can send a person out. We have been called out to look at tracks and such and it has always ended up being something else."

While the DNR has never had cause to investigate a Dog Man sighting, Schaefer said, "We have had some exotic cats."

Bob Wagner of the Tuscarora township police department serving the Indian River area (which Godfrey identified as another hot spot for Dog Man sightings) said his department has never had a report of the Dog Man, either.

"I've been doin' police work in this county for the last 32 years, and I've never heard of one sighting," he said.

Whether there really is a Dog Man stalking the woods of Michigan doesn't seem to matter much to Kathryn. She just doesn't want it near her house.

"I won't walk down there ever again," she said of the area where she saw the creature. "I used to take walks down there at night, but I won't do that now."

Simon Thalmann: Writer and copy editor in Kalamazoo, Michigan. His work has appeared in newspapers and literary journals.

FATE July-August 2009

THE WEREWOLF STATE
Daniel J. Wood

Myths and the anecdotal evidence of eyewitness testimony have preserved traditions about several mysterious creatures in the Wolverine State, none more terrible than the werewolf. For as far back as we can peer with the written word, we can make out the menacing, barely audible crunching of stalking paws in the Michigan snow. Occasionally, the werewolf leaves the depths of the primeval forest and pounces into our reality. Initially, the encounter leaves us stunned and stupefied. Similar reports flood the media, and our authorities struggle to come up with suitable explanations. In time, the public forgets the incidents until the next cycle begins.

Life imitates art
Michigan's last cycle of werewolf frenzy began in 1987. Steve Cook, hobby folklorist and production director at WTCM in Traverse City, composed a country-and-western song based upon stories he had collected of a wolf-like creature that walked upright and had no fear of humans.

According to Cook's research, the sightings began at a lumber camp near Big Rapids, Mecosta County, in the 1880s, although in his song, "The Legend," he changed the location to a camp in Wexford County. Cook tried to represent the folklore as accurately as possible, only occasionally altering details for the sake of producing a song. He told a reporter in the *Traverse City Record Eagle:* "The story deals with a creature that is very similar to the famous wolfman except we made it more homey by calling it a dogman." For dramatic effect – and looking forward to release on April Fool's Day, 1987, Cook's song warned that the dogman reappeared in the seventh year of each decade.

A dogman.

WTCM's listeners had already given "The Legend" a warm reception when, by happy coincidence, the unimaginable occurred: news reports announced that the Baldwin office of the Michigan Department of Natural Resources (DNR) had dispatched officers to investigate a mysterious animal attack on a cabin outside of Luther in Lake County.

According to *The Grand Rapids Press*, the DNR officers "found considerable damage to the screen and molding around a door and window. An animal had ripped into the screen and molding, apparently trying to get inside." After inspecting prints around the cabin, the officers ruled out bears and, instead, concluded that an unknown canine caused the damage.

The story echoed the plot of Cook's song, as well as accounts passed on in classic European lore. Michigan's werewolf woes went national. In "The Legend," Cook sang that, "Seven years past the turn of the century they say a crazy old widow had a dream of dogs that circled her house at night. They walked like men and screamed."

Also:

In '57 a man of the cloth found claw marks on an old church door.
The newspaper said they were made by a dog.
He'd a had to stood seven-foot-four.

Students of the occult could not help calling to mind a passage in Sabine Baring-Gould's classic 1865 study, *The Book of Werewolves*, where he cites Olaus Magnus' description of werewolf ravages in the Baltic: "... for when a human habitation has been detected by them isolated in the woods, they besiege it with atrocity, striving to break in the doors, and in the event of their doing so, they devour all the human beings, and every animal which is found within."

"The Legend" took off to become WTCM's most requested song, and folks from as far away as Germany asked how they might obtain a copy. Even radio personality Paul Harvey commented on the Michigan dogman after the wires picked up the story nationally. Locals began making their way to the Luther cabin to see the damage for themselves, some too frightened to leave the safety of their vehicles. On the downside, the Traverse City Chamber of Commerce began fielding calls not only from curiosity seekers but also from potential tourists who wanted some assurance that the area was still safe for vacationers.

As time wore on, the current went underground but never disappeared. When accounts of a similar (if not identical) creature from across Lake Michigan made national headlines early in 1992, Steve Cook contacted Wisconsin-based reporter Linda S. Godfrey and shared his observations and database. Godfrey, in turn, included substantial Michigan information in her 2003 chronicle of the Wisconsin werewolf, *The Beast of Bray Road*.

Dogmen of memory

Because of the werewolf sensations in Michigan and Wisconsin in the late 1980s and early 1990s, sources that might have been lost or forgotten over time became documented and easily accessible. Ordinary people contacted Cook, Godfrey, and others to tell extraordinary stories of their families' experiences with a wolf-like creature that could walk on two legs and possessed an evil, leering stare.

Robert Fortney was one such individual. Hearing "The Legend" on the radio motivated Fortney to allow reporters to document his own strange encounter, which took place in 1938, the year Fortney graduated from high school. Fortney was target shooting on the banks of the Muskegon River, near Paris, northwest Mecosta County, when a pack of five wild dogs charged out of the woods and attacked him. Seeing no other choice, Fortney shot the lead dog as it lunged for him; appropriately, three of the remaining dogs retreated back into the woods. One animal, however, enormous and black, did not immediately follow its comrades; instead, it stood on its hind legs and stared back at Fortney. A reporter who interviewed Fortney in 1987 wrote that "the only dog that didn't run off reared up on its hind legs and stared at Fortney with slanted, evil eyes and the hint of a grin."

Fortney, then 68, remarked: "It scared the devil out of me .... I wouldn't want to call it a dogman. l wouldn't know what to call it."

Clarence Gillispie of Interlochen, a local historian, has collected a number of accounts from Manistee County which lend credence to neighboring counties' sightings. One of the strangest tales collected involved two men fishing at dusk on Claybank Lake. In the gloaming, the two men struggled to see what first appeared to be an unfortunate dog swimming toward their boat. As the creature neared, the horrified men saw that it had the head of a canine and the body of a man. In terror, they beat the thing back with their oars and made a hasty retreat. When later contacted by the *Traverse City Record-Eagle*, one of the percipients declined to give a full interview and simply stated: "I don't know what I saw. I don't want to go into it."

No less terrorized was a parking couple. Strange sounds interrupted their nocturnal pursuits, and, when they wiped away the fog clouding their windows, they saw a creature with a vulpine head and the body of a man peering back at them through the glass. The incident so traumatized the young man that he swore off parking permanently – we know he experienced a real fright!

Invisible guardians
David Kulczyk, in the spring 1996 issue of *Strange Magazine* (vol. I 5), added a brief personal testimonial to the lore of the Michigan werewolf as he introduced readers to the Witchie Wolves of the Omer Plains. As a youngster growing up along the Lake Huron shoreline in the mid-1970s, Kukzyk and his peers experienced invisible frights at the jaws of unseen canine tormenters.

As a teenage rite of passage, the young men of Pinconning High School would drive 20 miles north to brave the wilderness of the Omer Plains. Kulczyk described the local tradition as follows: "According to local Chippewa [a.k.a. Ojibway] legend, Witchie Wolves are invisible spirit dogs that guard the graves of ancient warriors, attacking anyone foolish enough to venture out at night on foot." Invisible canids knocked to the ground and set upon those who dared leave their automobiles, barking and snarling around the victim's head. Some kids were scratched or had clothing torn from their bodies; less frequently, the canids targeted the cars themselves as objects of wrath, scratching bodies and denting roofs.

Perhaps the most disturbing factor of a Witchie Wolf assault is the high-pitched barking laughter that seems to come from all directions at once. Kulczyk observed that he had seen "tough guys cry while telling of their experience." If these entities intended to keep intruders out, their efforts may be judged a success. Numerous better seasoned outdoorsmen opt to seek opportunities elsewhere rather than risk trespassing on the Omer Plains.

Kulczyk regarded the Witchie Wolves as spirit guardians of sacred Native American sites-specifically, graveyards. In this case, the local legend would appear to be an understated memory. True enough, the area has its fair share of graveyards, but none of any special significance exists near the Omer Plains. A Native American trail parallel to the Rifle River once ran right through the area known for disturbances, but we find the real archaeological treasures farther upriver, near the little town of Selkirk. There, in east-central Ogemaw County, an unknown group of Native Americans erected a series of four earthen enclosures within a mile and a half of Selkirk-two north of the town and two to the south. The largest of these, called Number 2, measures 300 feet east to west and 280 feet north to south. Enigmatic openings, or gateways, mark some of the enclosures; Number 4 appears almost as an unfinished square or rectangle.

The corridor of forts

These formations, among others, were first studied by the Smithsonian at the close of the 19th century and by the University of Michigan in 1923. W.B. Hinsdale, of the university's Museum of Anthropology, made a curious observation in his 1925 book *Primitive Man in Michigan*. Hinsdale noticed that the formations northwest of the Omer Plains occupied "the same tier of townships" as the spectacular earthworks 40 miles to the west, in Missaukee County. Any notion of a purely coincidental alignment vanished when other archaeologists noticed that a veritable chain of earthworks spanned the northern third of Michigan's Lower Peninsula, stretching across from the Rifle River in the east to Manistee County in the west.

Gerald Haltiner, an Alpena-based archaeologist, named the enigmatic grouping Michigan's "corridor of forts." Few archaeologists today, however, view these structures as defensive earthworks, though many were palisaded. Instead, they posit that the earthen enclosures hosted seasonal gatherings where ritualized trade occurred between hunter-gatherers and agriculturists. The corridor straddles what scientists call Michigan's interbiotic zone, the line marking the northernmost extent of successful maize growing.

The builders obviously expended a great deal of energy clearing huge trees and heaping up the earth needed to erect their ceremonial structures. They treated these spaces as sacred centers and left them swept clean after use, just as today's worshiper might tidy up a pew after church.

The Native American builders selected these sites for spiritual rather than practical reasons. They were not constructed upon high ground, near high-traffic trails, or even close to good sources of water. There is no evidence that they were meant to be found or even seen again after they fulfilled their specific purpose.

Shamanic energy centers

The overwhelming majority of Michigan's werewolf sightings take place just south of the eastern and western edges of the corridor of forts. The little hamlet of Luther and the Omer Plains, for instance, lie on virtually the same latitude. Can this just be coincidental? Or did powerful Native American shamans purposely place these creatures just outside ritual precincts with the intent of discouraging interlopers? According to this theory, the holy men would infuse a place with emotion; the environment itself would then store images to be "played back" after certain human emotions indicated that the sanctity of the site was threatened.

With the passage of centuries, our mental and spiritual orientations have been altered so radically that those unfortunates experiencing a "playback" have unwittingly triggered the shamanistic alarm system. Many of our monsters, it naturally follows, are actually subconscious projections, creatures that do not really exist in the physical realm but in the spiritual and psychological.

Let us return to the two men fishing in Claybank Lake. These gentlemen most likely had no idea that the area once comprised part of a larger Indian reservation; neither were they aware of the irregular earthworks located just north of their recreational fishing hole. But something in their psyches triggered a playback. All these sites were selected to take best advantage of the earth's natural energies, and, the greater the telluric power available, the more spectacular the playback. As more and more ceremonial centers are lost to neglect, weathering, and looting, playback fails when the magical mechanism is cut off from its power supply.

Michigan's werewolves could also be projections from living shamans, highly skilled and experienced practitioners of ceremonial magic. To accomplish such a transformation, the magicians first place themselves in a deep trance. Then they draw upon etheric material from outside themselves to build a body of transformation far more powerful and robust than the so-called "body of light" available through astral projection.

Practitioners of such staggering mental ability should be regarded as extremely scarce. However, French colonists in Michigan frequently associated lycanthropy with evil magic. Often, a cornered werewolf would vanish before the eyes of its pursuers – but not before leaving behind some sign of its provenance. For example, a French farmer troubled by a *loup-garou* in the Detroit area tried to end the monster's reign of terror with a bullet fashioned from the melted silver of a saint's medal. Unfortunately, he only managed to shoot off the creature's tail, which the local Indians kept as "a powerful fetish."

When the 18th-century Detroiters tracked the werewolf to a swamp, it left a demonic footprint behind on the rock upon which it was last seen standing. A similar story from French Mackinac claimed that a sulfur spring bubbled up where the werewolf disappeared.

French connection

The tales of the French raconteurs, however, must be taken with a grain of salt. Their main purpose was to provide entertainment over the course of long winter evenings, and scholars have established that a number of stories were brought to Michigan – then the *pays sauvage*, or savage land-from France or eastern Canada – and simply adapted to local conditions.

The Old World France from which colonial Michigan sprang was steeped in Europe's richest tradition of lycanthropy. At the same time as the above tales supposedly took place in Michigan's New France, a very real horror, the Beast of Gevaudan, terrorized the southern French countryside. Several papers, including the *Gazette de France* and England's London Magazine, chronicled the exploits of the hearty men bravely endeavoring to end the hyena-like beast's depredations. A detachment of dragoons tracked the Beast of Gevaudan for more than a month before a soldier, one M. Antoine, killed it.

The Tale of Sheem

Michigan's Algonquian Indians regarded shapeshifting in a more neutral light, and being a shapeshifter did not automatically make one an evil person. An example of this can be found in the voluminous writings of Henry Rowe Schoolcraft, who served first as an Indian agent in territorial Michigan from 1822-36 and then went on to become the state's Superintendent for Indian Affairs until 1841. The idea of capturing what he called Ojibway "lodge stories" consumed Schoolcraft, and he blazed trails in anthropology as a pioneer ethnographer. One story he recorded, the "Tale of Sheem," may be read either allegorically or as a reflection of genuine Ojibway belief.

The narrative describes the sad plight of a young boy, whose natural family abandons him because of their own selfishness. As the youth struggles to survive winter, a pack of wolves takes pity on him, provides him with food, and gradually begins to accept him as kin. The boy comes to increasingly identify with the wolves until he eventually transforms into a wolf himself. Schoolcraft provides a translation of the song in his 1856 "The Myth of Hiawatha." The sixth stanza reads:

> *Ah, ye wolves, in all your ranging,*
> *I have found you kind and true;*
> *More than man – and now I'm changing,*
> *And will soon be one of you.*

A true cryptid?

Perhaps the cold northern forests shelter some unknown canid, an uncatalogued animal. Given the abundance of wilderness in Michigan, this is entirely possible.

For decades, a debate has raged as to whether the Wolverine State enjoyed the dubious distinction of being named after an animal that never actually lived there. Lest anyone despair, the wolverine staged a comeback in 2004. The solitary, pugnacious creature made several confirmed appearances in the area known to Michiganders as "The Thumb," even graciously allowing himself to be photographed by a wildlife biologist in February. These sightings, have put to rest any notions of Michigan being anything other than the Wolverine State.

Michigan's experience with the elusive wolverine causes us to wonder whether other such fearsome creatures lurk behind the foliage of Michigan's north woods, as yet unrecognized by natural science. Perhaps Michigan could just as well be known as the Werewolferine State.

Daniel J. Wood: Summa cum Laude graduate in European history and author of articles on religion, history, and archaeology.

FATE February 2005

THE BEAST OF BRAY ROAD'S FIRST APPEARANCE
Len Faytus

The Beast of Bray Road first came to light in southeastern Wisconsin when The Week ran an article by Linda S. Godfrey on the last Sunday of December 1991. The article described a werewolf-like creature that had been recently seen on Bray Road just east of Elkhorn, north of Lakeland Hospital and the old county poor farm and insane asylum.

Almost immediately, it became the topic of local conversation which commonly led to jocular speculation by armchair theorists that it was the result of a strange experiment at the county hospital. Others felt that the logical answer was an escapee from the insane asylum which had been closed for decades or a deformed dog or coyote that walked on two legs. The sheriff's department suggested the latter as the most reasonable explanation of the phenomena. For numerous reasons, that particular theory was the most ludicrous suggestion of all.

Dozens of witnesses claimed to have seen the werewolf throughout the 1980s and 1990s. Sightings were especially concentrated on Bray and Bower roads, Highway 11 between Elkhorn and Delavan, and La Grange Township, all in Walworth County. The beast was also seen, however, in a large 25-mile belt, a wide corridor stretching from Geneva Lake to the small city of Jefferson, 32 miles to the north. Some sightings were reported in Rock County to the west. To the northeast, the beast was sighted throughout the Kettle Moraine State Forest area and into Waukesha County and as far as Holy Hill in Washington County. The entire area alternated between farmland, dense woods, and impassable swamps.

Linda Godfrey, the premiere beast expert of Wisconsin, reported that Mark Schackelman had seen the creature twice at St. Coletta, which was a Catholic convent east of Jefferson, in 1936. It was messing around

A view down Bray Road. Photo by Len Faytus.

with an ancient burial mound and he stated that it was "straight out of hell." The Hebron area in Jefferson County was also a hotbed for sightings.

By most accounts, the Beast of Bray Road was man-sized at 150 to 200 pounds, standing five to six feet tall when erect. Witnesses described it as being covered in fur, barrel chested, with a wolf-like face with pointed ears. It possessed a bushy tail and canine legs. The beast was seen eating road kill, chasing down deer, and actually kneeling.

Showing little fear of humans, the creature eerily stalked witnesses on several occasions in a menacing fashion. Reportedly, it had high shoulders with a downward sloping back like a hyena when it was on all four legs and could glide both swiftly and smoothly on four legs. Surprisingly, it was also observed walking and running quickly on two legs. As a biped, the werewolf's gait was odd but not ungraceful. It was powerful, and the beast was not just nocturnal as it was also seen during the day.

Similar sightings have been reported in states such as Michigan, Tennessee, Illinois, Pennsylvania, Virginia, and Georgia where it was known by different local names. In Tennessee, there were reports of its violent appearance in the 1800s. Native Americans called it Windigo. The fairly recent appearance of the Chupacabra and its subsequent sightings, appear to almost describe the same animal, especially those reported in historic times.

The Beast makes an appearance in Geneva Woods

With all the recent sighting of the werewolf in southeastern Wisconsin, you may wonder if the creature is of recent vintage or was the animal also sighted in the past by early pioneers? The answer is that it was indeed seen in the region in earlier times and was first documented in 1857.

The affair took place eight months before the county's first murder when Richard Pierce had shot and killed David Hamilton at a small charivari outside of Whitewater. Pierce had retained two lawyers for his defense, Asa W. Farr of Geneva and 26-year-old Newton S. Murphy. Murphy lived at the Whitewater Hotel across from the train depot and kept an office on Center Street, Whitewater, at the Metropolitan Block. The defense lost the case at the trial and Pierce was given a life sentence. More important for us however is the correspondence that Murphy received from his brother F. S. Murphy in June 1857.

The letter described strange events that had recently occurred in Geneva Township, which was located 17 miles southeast of Whitewater and 6 miles south of Bray Road. There had been an unusual occurrence at the 64.25-acre homestead of 33-year-old John Deignan. The farm was one mile east of what is now Schofield Road on the north side of Highway 50, on the edge of the large and then still wild Geneva Woods, between Como and Geneva lakes.

The forest consisted of old growth oak that had occupied half of the township, encompassing some 18 square miles. At one time it surely covered some 200 square miles and was first described in 1831 by Mrs. John H. Kinzie who accompanied her husband and a small party from Fort Dearborn to Fort Winnebago. Somewhat provocatively, Geneva Lake, which was called Kish-wa-ke-ta, roughly "crystal water" by the Potawatomie, was known as Big Foot

Lake by early settlers. The name hints of Sasquatch but actually and much less mysteriously referred to Chief Big Foot. He had migrated to western Kansas with his entire village from the headwaters of the lake, now Fontana, in 1836.

The strange abduction of Catherine May Deignan

John and his wife, 31-year-old Ann Flynn Deignan, had emigrated from Ireland and were just starting their family. Their daughter Catherine May was born in nearby Bloomfield Township a few years earlier on April 23, 1854. Her younger brother John was born in 1856. The family's frightening experience began late in May. At the time, the homestead was still surrounded by forest. On Friday morning, May 29, three-year-old Catherine was seized from the threshold of the Deignan home by a large and ferocious looking animal which had emerged from the shadows of the woods.

It immediately took off with the girl, heading back towards the dense cover. The frantic screams of her mother caused the fierce animal to drop Catherine after she had been carried some 50 to 100 feet. Incredibly, this was the second time that the animal had appeared and taken the girl. On Tuesday morning, May 26, it had come out of the woods and snatched Catherine from the front yard of the homestead. The animal had succeeded in carrying her about 88 yards into the dark woods, in spite of the efforts of John and Anna to rescue their daughter, before it reluctantly let her go.

The animal that had twice grabbed the girl had been seen several times that spring by neighbors but always at a distance. Their isolated farms, which were hacked out of the forest, were surrounded by large tracts of woods. They did not know what kind of animal it was but recognized that it had little fear of humans. People that had not seen the animal firsthand assumed it was a bear, based on the descriptions given by the terrified family.

Eyewitnesses did not identify it as a bear, however. Furthermore, Murphy's letter to his brother implied that the creature grabbed the girl up in arms rather than by its mouth. The neighborhood was both alarmed and agitated by the event. Subsequently, a large party of determined township men hunted for the creature beginning on Wednesday, May 27, looking for its lair, but did not meet with success.

They planned to capture it if it was still in the area, which in 1857 meant that they planned to kill it. The sly creature unfortunately proved to be quite elusive. Kate, who survived the harrowing ordeal, never married. She died at Lake Geneva on the morning of January 15, 1896 of consumption, outliving her father by 12 years. Interestingly, her younger brother John who was alive during the abductions had died in 1889. The last person to witness the abduction firsthand, Anna Deignan, died on April 25, 1902. The farm remained in the family until the early 1990s.

Another early appearance of the beast

On November 5, 1869, a very similar strange-looking animal was seen by farmers, east of Janesville, on the Delavan Road, now Highway 11. It had been seen for a few evenings and was described as being very ferocious. It had fearlessly attacked some large and rough farm dogs. From appearances, the local farmers suggested that it looked like it was capable of quickly devouring a good-sized boy. Once again, non-witnesses proposed that it was also a bear, a suggestion scoffed at by those that had seen it.

Other rare animals

People of the 19th century generally knew a bear when they saw one, especially rural folk. In the late 1830s, early pioneers had shot numerous black bears in the area, some quite large. A real bear was spotted in Perry Township, Dane County, a few times over a 12-day period in 1866. A dozen men were organized to capture it and on a drive on September 30, Ole Halverson shot it with a .58 caliber Minnie ball, from an army musket. The bear weighed 400 pounds.

Other uncommon animals also wandered into the area on occasion. On the afternoon of July 29, 1867, August Hager, a 43-year-old Prussian, killed a large wildcat in some bushes near the Crawfish River bridge, about one mile from Jefferson, with two shots. It was three feet long and two feet tall. Three men, Lorenzo Dow Abbey, 48, his brother-in-law William Carnes, 44, and son-in-law James M. Burnham, 33, killed an enormous lynx with the help of a couple of boys including 13-year-old George Abbey on June 22, 1868.

The boys had seen it cross an open field on the William Harnden farm in Hebron Township, Jefferson County, just 16 miles north of Bray Road. Dogs were used to pursue it and after a severe fight with the dogs it took to the trees. Shot had no effect on it and it took a rifle slug to the head to capture him. He was five-and-half feet long, measured two feet nine inches high, and had black tasseled ears. Although the bear, wildcat, and lynx had not been native to the area for decades, the farmers knew what they were and never described them as strange unknown creatures.

Early mention of Bigfoot

The creature was more than likely not a Bigfoot type creature either. Bigfoots had been seen periodically in the Midwest and were not described as strange creatures but as large hair-covered wild men. One sighting appeared in the Jefferson Banner on July 15, 1868. The paper stated that another wild man had been seen, in this case, on the Manitou Islands in Lake Michigan. The wild man was eight feet tall, covered in hair, with a heavy brow. It was explained that the wild man was probably a four-year-old boy that had grown up there. There was a rumor that he was lost there about 20 years earlier. Plainly, people of the era attempted to rationalize what was seen.

Wolves, cougars, and weirder things

Curiously, several animals have made reappearances in the area in recent years. Lone male wolves that were eradicated since WWI have been seen, albeit mainly found dead on the highways. Black bears also occasionally lumber down from the north. An image of a bear was captured near Delavan in 2011 and authenticated. I myself saw a dead cub on Highway 12/18 in 2010 a few miles west of Cambridge in southeastern Dane County.

More than one cougar has been sighted in this part of the state too, verified by the Department of Natural Resources. In addition, a half dozen years ago, there were many reported sightings of the more paranormal black panther along Turtle Creek within the eastern city limits of Beloit, 27 miles to the southwest of Elkhorn. The creek, surrounded by dense woods and undergrowth, flows from Turtle Lake, midway between Whitewater and Delavan. Many of the witnesses were credible. One witness in those sightings was a Beloit schoolteacher.

I accompanied an APHIS wildlife specialist late in January 2009 on his niece's Watertown Township farm. The federal specialist was investigating the slaying of a horse named Ginger. A second mare, Big Mama, survived the predawn barnyard attack, 50 yards from the farmhouse. In that case, the agent determined that that it was an example of canine, possibly wolf, depredation.

The Wisconsin DNR, on the other hand, remained convinced that the culprit was a rogue cougar. Interestingly, a lone set of canine tracks were found at the scene. While the prints were definitely large enough to be wolf tracks, the gait was more like that of a domestic dog. While no plausible explanation was forthcoming, the incident did have elements to suggest some other creature was involved.

The Watertown affair seemed strangely reminiscent of another incident described by Godfrey that also occurred in Jefferson County, over three decades earlier. In that event, which took place near St. Coletta in 1972, a creature had been seen walking in a barnyard. Two weeks later it had caused pandemonium at the farm by shaking the screen door and leaving a 30-inch slash wound in a horse's neck. It was investigated at the time by the DNR. Accounts of that creature tended to suggest it was a Bigfoot rather than werewolf.

Both of the above-mentioned incidents involved physical confrontations with an unknown predator and possessed elements more related to the Deignan affair than to most sightings. The majority of Beast of Bray Road encounters were not physically aggressive although, many times, the animal was aggressive in nature. Many witnesses have reported to be frightened or threatened during their encounters but were not actually attacked.

Ever elusive

The Beast of Bray Road was indeed actually seen by early pioneers, who attempted to hunt it down after it snatched up a young girl. The pioneers were quite skilled in woodcraft but were unable to kill it, not surprisingly. Undeniably, the werewolf is never seen by the large numbers of modern hunters that traverse the countryside during deer season either. No lair, hair, or other evidence has ever been discovered.

Skeptics propose that for these reasons the beast does not exist or is the creation of hoaxers. The idea that it is a hoax would imply logistics over a great length of time that would be unsustainable. A prankster, furthermore, would be risking being shot by a 30.06 or 12-gauge slug for his or her efforts in this mostly rural area. Not much fun and definitely not worth the risk.

Perhaps the answer lies more in the paranormal although when it is seen, it appears to consist of real flesh and blood. Not that the creature really cares what humans believe anyway. It is as resilient as the *Jeepers Creepers* bat-like monster of movie infamy that was also described as coming "straight out of hell."

FATE website 2013

AN INTERVIEW WITH LINDA S. GODFREY
Brad Steiger

As an incurable collector of werewolf encounters and the author of *The Werewolf Book: An Encyclopedia of Shapeshifting Beings*, I was familiar with the eerily fascinating reports of werewolf sightings in Wisconsin that reached the national press in the early 1990s. The so-called "Beast of Bray Road" was pursued from the very beginning of its materialization in Elkhorn, Wisconsin, by journalist Linda S. Godfrey, who doggedly attempted to track the alleged werewolf to its lair.

In 2003, I was delighted when Prairie Oak Press sent me the galleys of Godfrey's book *The Beast of Bray Road: Tailing Wisconsin's Werewolf*, and I was pleased to write an enthusiastic blurb for the back cover. Subsequently, my wife and I developed a regular correspondence with the Wisconsin author, artist, and researcher of the strange, and Linda and I appeared that fall in *Fangs vs. Fiction*, a documentary on werewolves and vampires for American Movie Classics television channel. When I learned that Linda had received so many additional reports of werewolf and monster encounters that she could easily fill another book, I knew that FATE readers would want to know more

Linda S. Godfrey. Used with permission.

about the bizarre creature sightings in Wisconsin (for those wishing to report such a sighting of their own, Linda Godfrey's website is www. lindagodfrey.com).

The werewolf and the reporter

Brad Steiger: *The Beast of Bray Road* makes for an exciting and balanced reading experience because you employ the tools of a journalist, simply reporting the encounters with an alleged werewolf in an objective manner. When you have explored that technique, you become the researcher and examine the mystery from several facets. Although you brought the skepticism of the journalist to the early reports, you also admit that you have always been fascinated by the unexplained. Could this predilection have made you more responsive and curious when you heard the initial reports that there was a werewolf roaming the Wisconsin wilds?

Linda Godfrey: You're probably right that my lifelong interest in the weird side of life had much to do with my undertaking the investigation.

Part of the reason I ended up with that first newspaper story was that the other reporters wouldn't touch it with a 10-foot wooden stake. The newspaper editor was actually aghast and a little embarrassed when my story began making national headlines. That didn't stop them from selling a lot of t-shirts with my original "kneeling roadkill eater" sketch, however. To their credit, they did allow me to keep pursuing the story and add updates as events continued to surface. And a lot of newspapers would never have been openminded enough to have printed the original story in the first place.

But to my way of thinking, not only was it fascinating that people in my own town were reporting seeing a werewolf, it was news! This is not an everyday occurrence, and I felt the public had a right to know there might be something a little extreme slinking around.

Steiger: When you began your interviews with the witnesses, what struck you most about their encounters?

Godfrey: What impressed me most about the first witnesses was their almost visible sense of deep fright that was still obvious as they recounted what they saw. They didn't act like people making something up, and in fact, they could hardly bring themselves to tell their stories. I was also impressed by the fact that they all noticed a certain jeering cockiness from the creature as it made eye contact with them. This is a characteristic that has continued to be present in every sighting reported. Even when the witness is some distance away, he or she reports feeling almost more like the observed than the observer. And that is very unnerving to even the most macho, outdoorsy of the witnesses. I was also struck by the fact that the creature apparently was more interested in getting away than in harming anyone.

Steiger: How did you eliminate reports of what may have been perfectly natural sightings of wild or domesticated canines?

Godfrey: It's very possible that some of the sightings were of ordinary wolves or dogs. Officially, I don't eliminate any sightings that are reported in good faith, as long as the witness felt there was something very strange about it. In much Native American lore, spirit animals are visually indistinguishable from ordinary creatures. So if witnesses think there is something different enough about what they see that they are compelled to report it, I just put it down exactly as they tell it. I feel the more information we have, the easier it will be to see patterns.

It's worth noting that people do see ordinary dogs, coyotes, bears, wolves, et cetera all the time and the reaction is just, "Hey, there's a coyote," not, "Heaven help me, there's something so unusual it's scaring me to death!" So I tend to trust people's instincts when they say there was something not right about what they've spotted, whether it was size, speed, posture, or even as some have reported, telepathic communication!

The reports I do tend to eliminate are those where people report something very vague, such as a pair of yellow eyes in the ditch at night. Big deal; raccoons are everywhere. I've also learned to look askance at the few, very few, people who seem unduly excited about what they saw and are eager to present themselves as media stars. I've had two such incidents, but these are extremely rare and pretty easy to spot.

Real werewolves?

Steiger: Did you ever entertain the idea that the witnesses might have, indeed, seen a real werewolf?

Godfrey: The tough part about answering that question is defining "real" werewolf. Most people entertain the Hollywood notion of the slathering, tortured soul who transforms bodily under the full moon and must be killed with silver bullets. Others might consider the word to signify a shamanistic shapeshifter who is able to summon the very realistic illusion of another creature. Or perhaps you are talking about the medieval notion of a human who is able to project an astral entity that looks like a wolf (usually while the person is sound asleep) that is able to roam the countryside, kill and eat people, and that, if wounded, will transfer the wound to the corresponding area of the human body.

There are other versions, too. Statements by witnesses such as "I thought it was a demon from hell" or "it was something not natural, not of this world" have indeed made me wonder if something other than a natural, flesh-and-blood animal is roaming the cornfields around here.

A few witnesses I'll be detailing in my second book, *Hunting the American Werewolf*, claim to have seen the creature either morphing or materializing. This points to the supernatural, but still doesn't prove that an actual human has changed bodily structure, grown fur and fangs, and then sneaked out for a midnight possum dinner. However, I do consider the possibility. And while I know there are self-proclaimed lycanthropes who insist they do transmute, I haven't yet found the evidence to prove it occurs.

Steiger: Could any of the sightings have been of Bigfoot?

Godfrey: Several of the sightings, especially some of those that have come in since the first book was written, do sound more like a Bigfoot or Sasquatch than a wolfman or dogman. A few witness sketches have borne this out. They are still greatly in the minority, however.

It's interesting to me that every witness who has had a good look at the head has been adamant that it was either dog/wolf-like or ape-like. But since there do seem to be two separate types of sightings, we have to grapple with the unsettling fact that perhaps we have two different anomalous creatures in the vicinity. If natural animals, they would probably compete with each other for territory, water, and some food, and it's hard to believe a lot of them could exist in this relatively small area. If supernatural, though, there is no reason that one creature couldn't appear in different forms, and that would explain the creature diversity very neatly.

Steiger: How many of the sightings could have been pranksters in appropriate werewolf attire?

Godfrey: I don't believe any of the reported sightings that I've written about were hoaxes, with the exception of one person who claimed to have a second sighting, but I do know that there were a few unreported incidents on Bray Road involving pranksters.

After the first stories came out, there were a couple of young farm lads who had fun scaring some people on Bray Road by wearing Halloween masks. There was also a man renting one of the farms there who dressed up in a rather amateurish wolf or gorilla suit to scare away teenagers who were parking on his property, but I believe he only did that once or twice and then thought better of it.

These hoaxers were known around the Bray Road neighborhood, however, and their actions were limited. There is no way they could account for most of the sightings, the greater share of which happened far away from Bray Road. And since the bulk of sightings have been in very isolated places late at night or early in the morning, over many decades, the likelihood of a prankster accounting for more than a few incidents seems very slim.

Native monster lore

Steiger: I think you are familiar with the Native American legends of the Wendigo, a monster of the woods. Could there be a link between werewolf accounts, Bigfoot sightings, and some of these Native American traditions?

Godfrey: That's a very rich possibility and one I've been exploring with some of the native tribal people of Wisconsin. The Wendigo is often mentioned as an explanation for the Beast of Bray Road, but if you explore the many Wendigo legends, this particular story does not fit witness observations or the southern Wisconsin terrain very well.

The Wendigo legend is more related to starvation-related cannibalism in the northern forests, and varies widely in size and description from tribe to tribe. It's often composed of ice that melts down to reveal a human or animal. There are better fits, such as the Canadian Cree Hairy Heart beings that I talk about in my first book. The Hairy Hearts also sound like Bigfoot. But so far, the Native Americans I've talked with lean toward more of a "spirit being" explanation.

Steiger: Shapeshifting is an acknowledged and accepted device of tribal shamans. Could someone have mastered the craft of shapeshifting that has been an element of magick for thousands of years? Could ancient European magick traditions and practitioners have blended with the Native American legends to have created a hybrid monster?

Godfrey: This is another area I'm exploring in my second Beast book. But I'm not sure it would be necessary for ancient North American shamanic practices to blend with European magick to create this hairy creature; according to their own traditions, either society would be capable of such conjuring. In both medieval Europe and among our Native American medicine societies, it has been an accepted belief that animal forms could be created or summoned to our corporeal world by certain rituals and disciplines. Of course, these days there are various occultic groups blending what they know of native shamanism and other practices, sometimes with the involvement of psychotropic drugs, so it's hard telling what can be cooked up!

Steiger: What about some ghost, spirit, or multidimensional visitor having been responsible for the werewolf sightings?

Godfrey: Various paranormal researchers and writers have suggested that Wisconsin is a key "window area" with many portals from other dimensions. The latest superstring theories of quantum physics have posited that there must be at least 11 dimensions in our universe. Although we have no way of knowing whether "creatures" from one dimension could function in another (or if the other dimensions have anything we could recognize as life), it does make the idea that things could be popping in and out from other places a bit more plausible. And it would help explain the many sightings of UFOs, Bigfoot, oversized birds, ghostlike visions, light phenomena, and of course wolfmen, that keep paranormal researchers in this state hopping.

Steiger: You've mentioned that you have received so many new sightings of beasts in Wisconsin that you are planning another book on the subject. How do these accounts compare or contrast with the original sightings?

Godfrey: Not all of the sightings are new ones. Some go back 20 years, but some are as recent as this fall. Only a couple are from the Bray Road vicinity; the rest are scattered across southern Wisconsin, with a few incursions into the northern counties and other states, as well. I've been surprised at the number of them. People would approach me at library talks or book signings and say that they had been keeping the secret of their sightings for years, but once they saw the book and realized other people had seen the same thing, they finally felt they could talk about it.

Most of the sightings are very similar to the confrontations already published in terms of the way the creature looks and acts, but there have been some interesting deviances. As I mentioned earlier, a few of the witnesses have sketched something that looks more like Bigfoot, and there have been a few sightings that indicate paranormal origins. One thing I want to emphasize is the wide territorial range that is now apparent. Bray Road was only the locale where the first witnesses to come forward happened to live, and the site of a cluster of incidents. It no longer serves as the Beast's official street address, however. The two most recent sightings that I know of were in Madison and near Sharon (almost at the Wisconsin/Illinois border).

UFO connection?

Steiger: Has anyone – or have you – made any alleged link with extraterrestrial visitors to explain the sightings?

Godfrey: Attempts to link Beast sightings to UFO activities have been made by a few writers, based mostly on a comment I made around that same time of the Bray Road appearances, that an Elkhorn businessman had told me he and his son witnessed two strange lights in the sky. That's a pretty tenuous, circumstantial association. People are always seeing strange lights around Wisconsin; after all, we have three cities claiming to be the state's UFO capital. UFO sightings occur regularly all over the state, and are far more numerous than Beast sightings. (See the excellent Web site www.ufowisconsin.com for more info.)

The Beast and UFO sightings clusters do not seem to correlate in any significant way as far as I've been able to tell. We have a tremendous number of UFOs in northern Wisconsin, for instance, while the Beast sightings tend to concentrate more in the southern half of the state. Still, it's something I'll continue to look at.

Steiger: Driving through some of those deeply wooded areas of Wisconsin at night, after visiting the late August Derleth at Arkham House, I felt I could sense the same entities that Derleth and H. P. Lovecraft summoned watching me from the shadows. What makes Wisconsin so weird and haunted?

Godfrey: This state possesses a psychic atmosphere that crackles with mystique for anyone even slightly sensitive to these things; perhaps that is one of the reasons Wisconsin has produced so many great writers, too; Derleth and Zona Gale to name a couple from the past, and on up to Dennis Boyer, Jane Hamilton, and Michael Perry today. Each in his or her own way has been able to sense the vitality of this land, and to convey a spiritual connection to it. All anyone need do is walk around. Some of the oldest rock deposits in the world are found here, and the feeling that very ancient "things" still inhabit every glacial scoop and oak savanna is pervasive. There are lakes filled with water spirits and rivers known as death traps by the old loggers who once prodded lumber through their rapids. Wisconsin is also shaped by two of the stormy Great Lakes, replete with legends of shipwrecked ghosts and maritime phantoms.

Another influence is our strong history of Native American occupation. This state contains nearly all of the mysterious animal-shaped effigy mounds in the world within its borders. (I have been conducting studies of these and do find a correlation between these and the Beast sightings.) We have an ancient archaeological park, Aztalan, that features massive earthen pyramids. The state is encrusted with marvelous rock formations that have been used as ceremonial centers for millennia, and our great, deep stretches of piney woods could shelter any number of cryptozoological wonders. Throw in the traditions that our settlers imported from a jumbled mélange of Old Europe, and you have a perfect recipe for weirdness.

My most recent project has been a book titled *Weird Wisconsin: Your Travel Guide to Wisconsin's Best Kept Secrets and Local Legends* (Barnes & Noble, May 2005). Co-author Richard Hendricks and I had no problem stuffing the pages full of the strangeness of this state, in fact, we couldn't come close to fitting it all in. If any place in all the world was fated to become known as the locus of werewolves, it makes wacky sense that the place would be Wisconsin.

Brad Steiger: Writer and author who deals with the strange and unknown.

FATE May 2005

SHAPESHIFTERS AND THOUGHTFORMS

BERSERKIR AND OTHER RAGING SHAPESHIFTERS
Rosemary Ellen Guiley

In Norse lore, the *berserkir* are men of superhuman powers who go about with bearskins or wolfskins over their armor, and who are capable of demonic rage. In folklore, the *berserkir* ("men in a bear shirt") possess the ability to shapeshift into wolves, thus making them a type of werewolf.

In earlier times, the *berserkir* took advantage of feudal law in Norway. They roamed about the countryside challenging farmers to combat. According to law, if a man declined such a challenge, he had to forfeit his property to the challenger. If the farmer fought and was killed, the *berserkr* (singular) could seize his wealth. Thus, *berserkir* were widely feared in the countryside.

They were known to invite themselves to local feasts, where they would slay anyone who displeased them, often by snapping the backbone or splitting open the skull.

The *berserkir* were valued as warriors, for they were reputed to be able to work themselves into frenzies of madness or demoniacal

153

possession which gave them superhuman powers and insensibility to pain. Author Sabine Baring-Gould gives this description in his *The Book of Werewolves* (1865):

> *No sword would wound them, no fire burn them, a club alone could destroy them, by breaking their bones, or crushing in their skulls. Their eyes glared as though a flame burned in the sockets, they ground their teeth, and frothed at the mouth; they gnawed as their shield rims, and are said to have sometimes bitten them through, and as they rushed into conflict they yelped as dogs or howled as wolves.*

The rages were always followed by periods of extreme exhaustion.

Berserkir diminished as Christianity advanced through Europe. The characteristics of their frenzies, rages and superhuman strength are ascribed to werewolves. From their name comes the term "berserk," for frenzied, uncontrolled behavior.

Warrior and berserker. Swedish illustration pre-1905.

The eigi einhamr

In Nordic and also Icelandic lore, the *eigi einhamr* ("not of one skin") were a pagan cult of were-animals. The *eigi einhamr* men had the ability to transform themselves into animals and take on the form *(hamr)*, powers, and characteristics of those creatures. The transformed and empowered man was called *hamrammr*.

The shapeshifting was accomplished by donning the skin of the animal and going into a cataleptic trance. The astral body of the man left his physical form and entered the animal form. Another means of transformation was through magical incantation. The original form of the man remained the same, but those who saw him were bewitched to perceive the form of an animal.

The *eigi einhamr* retained his human intellect while an animal. If changed into a wolf, he went on a "wolf-ride" ravaging animals, humans and property.

Sergeant Bertrand

In the 19th century, a Frenchman who delighted in digging up and tearing apart corpses led to comparisons to the *berserkir*.

In 1848, a mysterious series of grave desecrations took place in Paris, including at the prestigious Pere la Chaise cemetery. Graves were found opened and the corpses torn to pieces and left lying about. At first it was thought that animals were to blame, but then human footprints found at the scene told police that a person, probably deranged, was responsible. Watches were set up at Pere la Chaise, but no culprit was captured, and the desecrations soon ceased.

In March 1849, the perpetrator struck again at the cemetery of S. Parnasse, setting off a spring gun trap. Guards rushed to the scene in time to see a man in military garb leap over the cemetery wall and escape. He left behind a trail of blood, indicating that he had been wounded by the spring gun. Police also found a bit of clothing torn from the man's military mantle.

Police went from barracks to barracks searching for a man with gunshot wounds. They were able to find and arrest the culprit, a junior officer in the 1st Infantry regiment, by the name of Sergeant Bertrand. He was hospitalized, and after he recovered from his wounds he was tried by court martial. He made a complete confession.

Bertrand said he had entered the army at age 20, following his education at the theological seminary of Langres. He was known among his companions as a refined, gentle fellow, though prone to fits of depression.

In February 1847, a peculiar madness seized him. He was out in the countryside walking with a friend when they came upon a churchyard cemetery. The day before a woman had been buried, but the grave had not been completely filled in due to a rainstorm. As he looked at the grave and the sexton's pick and shovel lying beside it, he was overcome by an intense desire to dig up the corpse.

Bertrand made excuses and got rid of his friend. He sneaked back to the churchyard and exhumed the body. He testified:

> Soon I dragged the corpse out of the earth, and I began to hash it with the spade, without well knowing what I was about. A laborer saw me, and I laid myself flat on the ground till he was out of sight, and then I cast the body back into the grave. I then went away, bathed in a cold sweat, to a little grove, where I reposed for several hours, notwithstanding the cold rain that fell, in a condition of complete exhaustion. When I rose, my limbs were as if broken, and my head weak. The same prostration and sensation followed each attack.
>
> Two days after, I returned to the cemetery, and opened the grave with my hands. My hands bled, but I did not feel the pain; I tore the corpse to shreds, and I flung it back in the pit.

Bertrand suffered no more episodes until four months later, when his regiment was sent to Paris. One day he went walking through Pere la Chaise, and suddenly a violent urge to dig up a corpse and tear it up came upon him again. That night he returned to the cemetery and exhumed the corpse of a seven-year-old girl, tearing her in half. A few days later, he dug up a woman who had died in childbirth, and had been buried only 13 days earlier. On November 16, 1848, he dug up a 50-year-old woman, tore her to pieces, and rolled himself in the bits.

Bertrand gave numerous similar accounts of other desecrations he committed. At first these attacks came after he drank wine, but later they came upon him without noticeable cause. Bertrand dug up both men and women, but he only mutilated female corpses. Sometimes he hacked the corpses to pieces with a spade, and other times he tore them with his teeth and nails. He tore mouths open to the ears, opened stomachs and pulled off limbs.

Bertrand said that during his hospital stay he had not felt any urges to continue his savage behavior, and he considered himself cured. The authorities evidently believed him, for he was given the light sentence of a year in prison.

The suddenness of his rage to rend corpses, followed by extreme exhaustion, was characteristic of *berserkir* behavior, and also of the medical symptoms found in lycanthropy.

Dracula and Bersicker

Bram Stoker, the author of *Dracula*, was acquainted with the folklore linking vampires and werewolves. When Jonathan Harker goes to Count Dracula's castle and meets the count, he is struck by animal-like characteristics, including bushy brows that nearly meet in the middle of the forehead – one of the tell-tale signs of a werewolf. The count also has hairy palms and long, pointed nails that are almost like claws.

Count Dracula is most memorable for his shapeshifting into a bat – a fictional invention of Stoker's – but he also shapeshifts into wolf form. The count takes passage on a ship bound for England. En route, he vampirizes the crew and kills them, and the derelict ship crashes into the harbor at Whitby, England. Witnesses see what appears to be a wolf or a huge dog that leaps from the ship and disappears into the landscape.

Dracula also has command over wolves. He tells Harker that the howling wolves in the forests around the castle are "the children of the night."

"Bersicker," a variation of *berserkir*, is the name of a Norwegian wolf that runs amok when he is recruited for an errand by the count after the vampire comes to England.

Stoker's notes show that the source for the creature and his name was inspired by *The Book of Were-Wolves* by Sabine Baring-Gould, which describes a *berserkr* (singular) as "a man possessed of superhuman powers, and subject to accesses [sic] of diabolical fury."

In *Dracula*, an article attributed to the *Pall Mall Gazette*, dated Monday, September 18, relates the story of the wolf, which escaped from the Zoological Gardens in London (now the London Zoo, located in Regent's Park in north London).

According to the keeper, Thomas Bilder, Bersicker is one of three grey wolves from Norway that had arrived at the gardens four years earlier. Bilder described Bersicker as "a nice well-behaved wolf, that never gave no trouble to talk of." He said that on the afternoon of September 17, the wolf went crazy and began tearing at its bars as if it wanted to get out. Bilder noticed a strange man nearby: "...a tall thin chap, with a 'ook nose and a pointed beard, with a few white hairs runnin' through it. He had a 'ard, cold look and red eyes, and I took sort of mislike to him, for it seemed as if it was 'im as they was hirritated at." It was, of course, the count. Bilder noticed that the man wore white gloves, which, unbeknownst to him, hid the count's hairy palms and pointed nails.

The man suggested to Bilder that the wolves were upset, and he smiled with "a mouth full of white, sharp teeth." While they talked, the wolves settled down. Bilder stroked Bersicker's ears, and so did the stranger, saying he was used to wolves. When the man left, Bersicker watched him until he was out of sight, and then laid down in a corner.

When the moon rose later, all the wolves began howling. Bersicker was discovered escaped, with the bars to his cage bent and broken. He reappeared the following day around noon, docile and calm, but with his head cut and full of broken glass, as though he had gone over a wall topped with a defense of broken bottles. He was locked up in his cage.

According to Stoker's notes, he evidently intended to have a wolf captured and killed near the house of Dracula's first British victim, Lucy Westenra, whose health was failing as the vampire repeatedly drained her blood. Instead, Bersicker apparently was recruited by Dracula to attempt to breach the defenses around the house. On the night of Bersicker's escape, Lucy is frightened by flapping at her window, and also the howling of what she takes to be a dog – though the howling is much fiercer and deeper than a dog's – in the shrubbery outside the house. She gets up and looks out the window, but sees only "a big bat, which had evidently been buffeting its wings against the window."

The episode with Bersicker reinforces Dracula's affinity with wolves, and his ability to command them.

DION FORTUNE'S ECTOPLASM WEREWOLF
Rosemary Ellen Guiley

I s it possible to create a werewolf from thought? One of the most famous occultists and magical practitioners of the 20th century, Dion Fortune, discovered how her own chaotic, angry thoughts and emotions created a real and dangerous supernatural creature.

Fortune is best-known as an expert on psychic attack, and her book, *Psychic Self-Defence*, published in 1930, still reigns as a classic, definitive work on the subject.

Born in England in 1891 as Violet Mary Firth, Fortune grew up a naïve, vulnerable, impressionable young woman who had to learn how to psychically fight for herself. Early in her working career, she fell victim to an abusive female boss who used magical techniques against her to break down her will and self-esteem, and manipulate her. Fortune left her job, and was a mental and physical wreck for three years.

Her experience caused her to research occultism to determine what had happened to her, and how she could have defended herself against it. "My body was like an electric battery that had been completely discharged," she wrote. "It took a long time to charge up again, and every time it was used before charging was completed, it ran down again rapidly. For a long time I had no reserves of energy, and after the least exertion would fall into a dead sleep at any hour of the day."

Her research led her to conclude that damage had been sustained by her etheric double, a nonphysical replica of the body which is attached to it and helps channel the universal life-force to it. It is part of the aura, or invisible energy field, that surrounds the body. Fortune believed that the damage to her etheric double caused by her abusive boss created a leak in her life-force. Thus, she suffered profound exhaustion and mental fatigue.

Fortune's turnaround came in 1919 when she took initiation into an occult order, the Alpha and Omega Lodge of the Stella Matutina. She adopted her pen name of Dion Fortune from her magical motto of the order, *Deo Non Fortuna* ("By God, not chance"). The Stella Matutina was an outer order of the renowned Hermetic Order of the Golden Dawn, the greatest, albeit short-lived, Western magical order in modern times. The Golden Dawn boasted such occult luminaries as Samuel Liddell Macgregor Mathers, Aleister Crowley, William Butler Yeats, Arthur Edward Waite and Israel Regardie.

Fortune was gifted psychically and mediumistically, and had a great talent for the magical arts. She witnessed bizarre phenomena and participated in psychic feuds, fending off psychic attacks in the name of the Masters of the Great White Lodge. As she wrote later, she "kept the occult vigil when one dare not sleep while the sun is below the horizon; and hung on desperately, matching my staying-power against the attack until the moon-tides changed and the force of the onslaught blew itself out." She worked as a psychiatrist, and attributed many of the symptoms in cases she saw to psychic attacks.

In 1924, Fortune departed Stella Matutina and founded her own order, the Community (later Society) of the Inner Light. She died in 1946.

The werewolf

Fortune had what she described as "an exceedingly nasty experience" in which she inadvertently created an ectoplasmic thoughtform werewolf.

She decided to tell the story in *Psychic Self-Defence* as an example of what can happen when a person plays with occult forces:

I had received serious injury from someone who, at considerable cost to myself, I had disinterestedly helped, and I was sorely tempted to retaliate. Lying on my bed resting one afternoon, I was brooding over my resentment, and while so brooding, drifted towards the borders of sleep. There came to my mind the thought of casting off all restraints and going berserk. The ancient Nordic myths rose before me, and I thought of Fenris, the Wolf-horror of the North.

Immediately I felt a curious drawing-out sensation from my solar plexus, and there materialized beside me on the bed a large wolf. It was a well-materialized ectoplasmic form... grey and colorless, and... it had weight. I could distinctly feel its back pressing against me as it lay beside me on the bed as a large dog might.

I knew nothing about the art of making elementals at that time, but had accidentally stumbled upon the right method – the brooding highly charged with emotion, the invocation of the appropriate natural force, and the condition between sleeping and waking in which the etheric double readily extrudes.

I was horrified at what I had done, and knew I was in a tight corner and that everything depended upon my keeping my head. I had had enough experience of practical occultism to know that the thing I had called into visible manifestation could be controlled by my will provided I did not panic; but that if I lost my nerve and it got the upper hand, I had a Frankenstein monster to cope with.

I stirred slightly, and the creature evidently objected to being disturbed, for it turned its long snout towards me over its shoulder, and snarled, showing its teeth. I had now "got the wind up" properly; but I knew that everything depended on my getting the upper hand

and keeping it, and that the best thing I could do was to fight it out now, because the longer the Thing remained in existence, the stronger it would get, and the more difficult to disintegrate. So I drove my elbow into its hairy ectoplasmic ribs and said to it out loud:

"If you can't behave yourself, you will have to go on the floor," and pushed it off the bed.

Down it went, meek as a lamb, and changed from wolf to dog, to my great relief. Then the northern corner of the room appeared to fade away, and the creature went out through the gap.

I was far from happy, however, for I had a feeling that this was not the end of it, and my feeling was confirmed when next morning another member of my household reported that her sleep had been disturbed by dreams of wolves, and she had awakened in the night to see the eyes of a wild animal shining in the darkness in the corner of her room.

Now thoroughly alarmed, I went off to seek advice from one whom I have always looked upon as my teacher, and I was told that I had made this Thing out of my own substance by revengeful thoughts, and that it was really a part of myself extruded, and that I must at all costs recall it and reabsorb it into myself, at the same time forgoing my desire to "settle accounts" with the person who had injured me. Curiously enough, just at this time there came an opportunity most effectually to "settle" with my antagonist.

Fortunately for all concerned, I had enough sense left to see that I was at the dividing of the ways, and if I were not careful would take the first step on to the Left-hand Path. If I availed myself of the opportunity to give practical expression to my resentment, the wolf-form would be born into an independent existence, and there would be the devil to pay, literally as well as metaphorically. I received the distinct impression, and impressions are important things in psychic matters, for they often represent subconscious knowledge and experience, that *once the wolf-impulse had found expression in action, the wolf-form would sever the psychic navel-cord that connected it with my solar plexus, and it would be no longer possible for me to absorb it.*

The prospect was not a pleasant one. I had to forgo my dearly-loved revenge and allow harm to be done to me without defending myself, and I also had to summon and absorb a wolf-form which, to my psychic consciousness at any rate, looked unpleasantly tangible. Nor was it a situation in which I could either ask for assistance nor expect much sympathy. However, it had to be faced, and I knew that with every hour of the Thing's existence it would be harder to deal with, so I made the resolution to let the opportunity for revenge slip through my fingers, and at first dusk summoned the Creature. It came in through the northern corner of the room again (subsequently I learnt that the north was considered among the ancients as the evil quarter), and presented itself upon the hearthrug in quite a mild and domesticated mood. I obtained an excellent materialization in the half-light, and could have sworn that a big Alsatian was standing there looking at me. It was tangible, even to the dog-like odor.

From it to me stretched a shadowy line of ectoplasm, one end was attached to my solar plexus, and the other disappeared in the shaggy fur of its belly, but I could not see the actual point of attachment. I began by an effort of the will and imagination to draw the life out of it along this silver cord, as if sucking lemonade up a straw. The wolf- form began to fade, the cord thickened and grew more substantial. A violent emotional upheaval started in myself; I felt the most furious impulses to go berserk and rend and tear anything and anybody that came to hand, like the Malay running amok. I conquered this impulse with an effort, and the upheaval subsided. The wolf-form had now faded into a shapeless grey mist. This too absorbed along the silver cord. The tension relaxed and I found myself bathed in perspiration. That, as far as I know, was the end of the incident.

I had had a sharp lesson, and a highly instructive one. It may not be convincing to other people, owing to the lack of corroborative evidence, but it was exceedingly evidential to me, and I put it on record for what it is worth to those who, having personal knowledge of these things, can see its significance.

It is a curious point that, during the brief twenty-four hours of the Thing's life, the opportunity for an effectual vengeance presented itself.

Thoughtform projections may have played roles in some of the historical cases of ravening werewolves. Fortune observed that at one point she felt overcome by violent urges herself. Perhaps some of the individuals who confessed to werewolfism had mental or emotional disorders that caused a thoughtform projection of energy, which in turn incited them to "go berserk."

ANOTHER LOOK AT WEREWOLFERY
Nandor Fodor

Man becomes wolf? Scientists have a name for this horrific phenomenon – *lycanthropy* – but that is about all they do have sincere werewolves have proved too elusive for scientific study. However, some years ago I received a complete report from perhaps the only scientific observer ever to witness a possible incident of man becoming animal.

Even this report does not present sufficient evidence to establish lycanthropy as either fantasy or reality.

If reality, we cannot determine from the report if it is a reality of biology or of psychology.

If fantasy, lycanthropy is unlike any other yet sprung from the mind of man because it credits were-man with a shapeshifting capacity which man in his evolution does not possess. Caterpillars dissolve their forms and become butterflies, polliwogs become frogs, but the only way man can surrender his human form is through death.

Were-man is thought to change his form, and unlike any other creature, he can reverse his shift. The butterfly can never again be a caterpillar, but a were-man freely shifts from man to animal and back.

If not biologically, at least psychologically we face a fascinating problem in werewolferie. A man tired of civilization may want to escape into a subhuman level of existence and gratify, without guilt and fear, his cannibalistic, necrophilic, orgiastic and criminal fantasies. Savages may add their own aspirations of stealth and strength of the beasts of the jungle.

It is to just such an animal-imitating savage group that we owe this unique first-hand account of lycanthropy. The report was written for me on March 23, 1933, by Dr. Gerald Kirkland, then a 37-year-old medical practitioner at Trellis, Glamorganshire, England, and formerly Government Medical Officer in Southern Rhodesia.

Hidden in the sheltering branches of a tree, he witnessed the jackal dance of the natives. Without any attempt at embellishing his account, I shall reproduce it here from his letter to me word for word:

"There are, in certain parts of Africa, animal dances. They are supposed to have deep and significant meanings. They are deadly secret and it is very hard to see them. I have seen two and to our eyes they are the most bestial, revolting and disgusting things that anyone could imagine. The practice of the Black Mass is child's play in comparison. I do not think myself that there is much beyond frightful perversion in them, but there may be. I leave it to you. Personally, I don't mind filth – in fact I'll challenge anyone to tell yarns of that nature against me but I have no time for bestiality, so if I tell you this as it occurred please realize that it is for the element of lycanthropy therein that I do so. Good. Prepare for revolting beastliness!

"In advance I must say that other observers have stated that there is no actual transformation, but the mimicry is so absolute that one has to take the greatest precaution not to be deceived. There it is, maybe so, I only know what I saw and I am not blind, though I admit to some psychic abilities. One man said to me: 'You know, the performers become so possessed and obsessed with the idea that they are animals that I have found it quite difficult to remember that they are not.' I think he spoke truer than he meant.

"This is what I saw: A clear moonlight, lovely night. In a clearing in the forest natives of both sexes sitting in a ring, women on one side, men on the other, eating stinking meat, and boozing, oh but BOOZING!! No native can do anything psychic, or even funny unless he is drunk (*mot sage*). When the required degree of drunkenness was attained the "fun" began.

"First there was an exhibition of sexual perversion such as would put the Continental *Exposition Orientales* on the level of a village party league, and always more and more booze. When at last, and this took a long time, the combined effort of love and liquor had transported the natives almost to bedlam, the Nanga stepped into the center of the ring and started to dance. As he danced, his voice became more and more animal like, till at last it was indistinguishable from that of a jackal in the rutting time. By this time all the natives were quite naked, limbos have been torn off (you can guess how). Jaws were hanging, most of the men were slavering and drooling at the lips like animals, they were crawling around and licking each other like dogs. Then the women howled the jackal love calls. Then the Nanga in an inhuman frenzy, fell to the ground and lay on his belly in the dust, squirming and jerking his limbs like one in an epileptic fit, and then lay still. Meanwhile there was a perfect mimicry of dogs (jackal) on the heat. I need not go into further details, there was nothing that animals do, including homosexuality and masturbation, that was not indulged in, with the appropriate noises.

"Then came the climax. The Nanga rose to his feet, performed a few more gyrations, then fell again frothing blood and saliva in a great stream. From outside the ring came jackal calls, so real that I twisted round my tree to see the dogs come in and a young girl (about 17 as I ascertained it afterwards) and a man crawled into the ring. Well, I can't tell you what they did. The other imitation was good but this was uncanny. I kept rubbing eyes and I felt horrible. I can't describe to you what I felt. There was a considerable amount of fear mixed with it. You will laugh at me if I call my feelings unearthly, certainly they were unpleasant when all of a sudden, and quite without warning, there were two jackals copulating in that circle. There was no doubt about it whatever in my mind, not the slightest I would swear they were jackals. There was the Nanga lying on his belly, unconscious. I am very tempted to say, in a trance and there were the jackals, they even went over and nosed at him once, with the well-known jackal curiosity. An important point to remember that they went on and on with their sexuality as dogs can, but no human. Finally, girl, jackal, whatever you like to call her, bit the male thing hard and they bounded up into the forest together. All the natives by now were "out to the wide." But soon after this, very significantly, the Nanga recovered. And that was that.

"There you are! What do you make of it? There was an aftermath which was interesting. Next day a young girl, 17 years of age, was brought in from the district, terribly exhausted and complaining of rape. I had to examine her. The parts were terribly lacerated, swollen and torn, while there were a series of scratches on her breasts and thighs. And what do you make of that!"

I would say that the scratches argue that when human beings behave like jackals, they scratch and bite like jackals.

As to what the doctor saw, it unquestionably belongs to the sexual pathology of savages. They wanted to change into jackals and accomplished this with a startling realism. The witch doctor, by his psychism, no doubt contributed a significant quota to their paroxysms. Whatever really happened was a highly pathological and regressive form of self-extension.

One additional series of reports by scientific observers should be included in this discussion of lycanthropy. There are the reports of the materialization of animals by the Polish engineer Franck Kluski. During the 1920's, Kluski's materializations were witnessed by some of the most astute scientists ever to probe psychic phenomena. Investigators including Prof. Charles Richet, Dr. Gustav Geley, Professor Pawlowski, and Mrs. Hewat McKenzie testified to the reality of the Kluski phenomena.

These materializations of apparently living animals are included as lycanthropic phenomena on the basis of the psychic claim that materialized phantoms are built from a substance exuding from the medium's body. Hence, it is part of the human organism that is transformed into an animal when an animal is materialized.

This series of reports may be considered to establish a prima facie case for a superbiology of the future in which shapeshifting may become a matter of enduring research.

At the Institute Metaphysic in Paris, through Franck Kluski, an apeman "materialized." Geley reported that its large, shaggy head was felt to press the right shoulder and against the cheek of a sitter. It was covered with thick, coarse hair. A smell came from it like that of a deer or a wet dog. There was also a materialization of a bird and a lion.

Of the bird, Professor Palowski reported "that it flew around, beating its wings against the walls and ceiling, and when it finally settled on the shoulder of the medium, it was photographed with a magnesium flash, as the camera had been accidentally focused on the medium and was ready."

The lion was described by Colonel Ocholowicz as follows:

"Accompanying him (an Oriental apparition) was a rapacious beast, the size of a very big dog, of a tawny color, with slender neck, mouth full of large teeth, eyes which glowed in the darkness like a cat's which reminded the company of a maneless lion. It was occasionally wild in its behavior, especially if persons were afraid of it, and neither the human nor the animal apparition was much welcomed by the sitters... The lion, as we may call him, liked to lick the sitters with a moist and prickly tongue, and gave forth the odor of a great feline; and even after the séance, the sitters, and especially the medium, were impregnated with this acrid scent as if they had made a long stay in a menagerie among wild beasts."

Beyond the question of facts or delusions, the Kluski reports call for many uncomfortable considerations. Human survival may be provided at considerable pain: do we have to face also the survival of animals? Or were these animal materializations ephemeral creations? If not, what happens to animal evolution after death? Having lost the inhibition of oral limitation, are they on the way to self-consciousness?

At this stage we can only pose such baffling questions. It is impossible to answer them. The scientific spirit would be satisfied with much less; a possible exploration, through shapeshifting, of the psychic life of animals, to know how they respond to life and what this mysterious world we inhabit is like to them.

Nandor Fodor (1895-1964): Psychical researcher, author, psychoanalyst, lawyer, and journalist best known for his pioneering theories on the sexual and psychological aspects of mediumship and poltergeist phenomena.

FATE January 1964

SKINWALKERS AND THE WITCHERY WAY
Christopher O'Brien

In August 2008, WEX head explorer David Hatcher Childress suggested that I should "write a book about skinwalkers," telling, me "cryptocreatures are big right now." I remember responding that it would be virtually impossible because very little has been written on the subject of skinwalkers and that it would be a challenge to attempt to write an in-depth magazine article on the subject – forget about a full-length book. But he did get me thinking; why not use the skinwalker as a boilerplate to examine his ancient uncles – the tricksters? So, what follows is an expanded examination of these legendary adepts adapted from my 2009 AUP book, *Stalking the Tricksters*.

One important element that seems to correlate tricksters' forms transculturally is the ability to shapeshift, and this ability is allegedly found among skinwalkers and other black adepts, as we will see. In 1993, I began documenting unexplained reports and researching the belief systems of the most local of the 13 tribes from three regional groups of Indians that visited the San Luis Valley. I concentrated on the Ute, Tewa, Diné (Navajo/Apache), and Pueblo Indians. I wanted to know: are there traditional interpretations that could help explain the region's UFO-type activity, or provide insight into the occult, or explain the strange, mysterious, and unusual cattle deaths?

This region of the continent is located just beyond the extreme northern extent of the earliest incursion into North America by Europeans. It is a place where indigenous belief has blended and melded with a unique brand of Catholic fundamentalism. Due to its isolation for generations, the 500 years of subcultural programming has slowly developed a blend of indigenous and western interpretation that give this subculture a unique set of superstitions and beliefs. This region is a superb sociological petri dish/melting pot of belief. This holds true especially around traditions of Native adepts who are said to be able to manipulate reality around the power of their will, for good or for evil purposes or for amoral trickery.

Depiction of a skinwalker.

Pueblo Indian beliefs

Skinwalkers are, by literal definition, a Diné tradition. Before we dive into the perilous world of the skinwalker, let's look at the concept of witchcraft in the Pueblo Indian's traditions where much of Diné knowledge and beliefs have been borrowed and culturally adapted since their arrival in the Southwest United States in the 12th and 13th century.

When it comes to witchcraft and witches, Pueblo Indians are today still highly suspicious of their neighboring pueblos. Belief in witchcraft is widespread and there are variations between tribal traditions that appear to exacerbate these suspicions. Generally, witches practice their craft secretly within their own pueblo. However, the fear of witches from outside Pueblos is very real. I have learned that a secret trial involving witchcraft within two pueblos is currently underway and this suggests that this "taboo" topic is still very much alive in modem pueblo society.

As I mentioned, shapeshifting seems to be a common thread that is found throughout most, if not all, Southwestern Native American traditions relating to witches' legendary abilities. These adepts allegedly are able to transform into a variety of animal forms and can also allegedly use various animals' body parts to transform some aspect of their humanness into that of a desired animal. Some accounts in the Northern Rio Grande pueblos mention the ability to change into fireballs, or "flaming bowls" when they need to travel somewhere extremely fast. I have received reports from terrified locals claiming to have seen fireballs that they report to me as "witches." Where are they going and what is their agenda? According to legend, these adepts are said to meet regularly in enclaves in caves or by large, isolated rock formations. In the San Luis Valley, there is a legend that witches have been meeting for hundreds of years at the "Witch Rocks" southwest of Sanford, Colorado. For decades, strange lights have been reported in the area. Florence Ellis relates what was commonly thought about pueblo witch society enclaves in the early 20th century.

Witch society meetings are thought to be held in the dead of night in a cave at some distance from the pueblo. The witches arise, slip outside quietly and change themselves into animals, coyotes, toads, dogs, crows, hawks, or other birds, to travel to the meeting in the cave. One tale relates the plight of a wife who left her human eyes in a cup in the house and used owl eyes, but when she returned in the early morning the human eyes had been found by her husband and dunked in urine, which made them forever unusable. Detail of what goes on in the cave are few because witches are not informants, and persons who do not belong to a ceremonial society never know proceedings of a society. According to Isletans, the secret witch meetings are held on a black mesa known as Shemtua, about five miles northeast of the pueblo, near the Los Padillas boundary line.

Navajo and Apache witchcraft

Beside the little-known information about Diné witchcraft and skinwalkers I have found in obscure self-published books from Navajo authors and from academic compilations, there are a few fleeting references to these black magician shapeshifters on the Internet. Skinwalkers are most frequently seen as a coyote, wolf, owl, fox, or crow and the *yeenaaldlooshii* is said to have the power to assume the form of any animal they choose. Witches use the form for expedient travel, especially to the Navajo equivalent of the "Black Mass," a perverted song (and the central rite of the Witchery Way) used to curse instead of to heal. They also may transform to escape from pursuers. Some Navajo also believe that skinwalkers have the ability to steal the skin or body of a person. The Navajo believe that if you lock eyes with a skinwalker they can absorb themselves into your body. It is also said that skinwalkers avoid the light and that their eyes glow like an animal's when in human form, and when in animal form their eyes do not glow as an animal's would.

During my 13-year field investigation/research project in the San Luis Valley (SLV) in south-central Colorado/north-central New Mexico that resulted in my *Mysterious Valley* book series, I gathered information from indigenous people about the strange goings-on that have apparently always blistered the magical four-corners region. Over the years I've noticed witnesses' personal bias and what appear to be subcultural preconceptions around these subjects. For instance, this bias included sub-cultural references to "witches" and "skinwalkers" when interpreting their sightings of "balls of light;" orbs or unusual individuals in their environment. However, whenever someone reported something weird and used traditional interpretations to explain the phenomenon they observed, I took extra notice.

Naturally I was intrigued by hints of information held by the local natives. There seems to be a strict taboo around speaking of those who practice the Witchery Way, and very few, if any Navajo will acknowledge the subject to outsiders. The paranormal.lovetoknow.com website has a very informative page on Navajo witchcraft, and they state:

> The four basic "ways" of Navajo witchcraft are "Witchery, Sorcery, Wizardry and Frenzy." None of the four are actually witchcraft in the European sense of the word. They are simply additional parts of the vast spirituality of the Navajo people. [W]itchcraft is not separate from Navajo spirituality, it is simply another set of "Ways" within the Navajo religion. The Navajo believe that people must live in harmony with Mother Earth, and that there are two classes of beings, Earth People who are mortals, and the Holy People who are unseen spiritual beings.

Most forms of this Witchery Way are apparently focused on corpses and death and the Navajo have a fervent avoidance of death.

Who is stalking whom?

In late 1998, a prominent member of the Crestone, Colorado, community where I lived approached me. She casually asked what I knew about "Indian witchcraft." The request was out of character and I instantly sensed something unusual was behind her low-key request. I related to her basic information pertaining to rituals of intent and protection, the use of power talismans and the like and she interrupted me, took me aside and told me about a strange adorned animal spine and skull bundle that had been found hanging by a creek behind her house. It seems she had recently experienced a falling out with a visiting Native American "medicine man" and then, some time later, this scary-looking bundle turned up near her house. She had quickly disposed of the bundle, making it impossible for me to study and make note of the objects and how they were arranged. It was difficult for me to translate or interpret, but I offered to conduct a cleansing and blessing at the spot where the scary-looking artifact was discovered. Several months went by and she never mentioned the event again, nor did I ever ask her for an update on the peculiar situation; some questions are better left unasked.

Some months later, I had moved out into the valley to a sentry-like, two-story house with a majestic view of the Sangre de Cristo Mountains three miles to the east. The house was equipped with a 500-watt solar energy system that would barely power my computer on a sunny day.

One evening, Wednesday, November 10, 1999, at 6:20 p.m., I was taking a shower in the attached greenhouse and noticed, with a start, what could only be described as an antler-adorned, six-foot tall, bipedal creature gliding across the front of the windows, from left-to-right. The being was in the shadow just out of the thin light projected out to the yard, but I was able to easily discern its distinctive shape.

I learned later that what I witnessed while taking a shower is eerily similar to Diné accounts of a skinwalker lurking about. But, reviewing my event log I am reminded of another weird incident that occurred the prior late summer/early fall. I had been sitting downstairs alone watching TV in the living room, when a rapid succession of rapping sounds circled the house around the walls of the second story above. The five or six raps banged in a clockwise circle around the house's upper story and I bolted outside with a flashlight to see whatever it was. Nothing. I made note of it but I'm still puzzled today – years later – what it could have been. While researching this chapter, I found that sounds of rapping around your house are attributed by some Diné as being a skinwalker attempting to get your attention! Okay...

What is a Skinwalker?

That blustery fall in the SLV, was I being watched (or haunted?) by a skinwalker? Probably not, but the curious synchronicities are worthy of mention. Skinwalkers are said to be evil sorcerers that exist alongside and among the Diné people. They are said to practice the "Witchery Way," be able to transform themselves into a variety of animal forms, and practice a particularly feared form of black magic. The actual term "skinwalker" comes from the Diné description "with it, he goes on all fours" or *yeenaaldlooshii*. This term refers to the skinwalker's alleged ability to change into a four-legged animal such as a coyote, wolf, fox or sometimes a bear. As a result of this belief, it is taboo to wear the skins of these carnivores. Sheepskin and calfskin are acceptable, but carnivore skin used for clothing is extremely frowned upon. In the Diné tradition, there are several different types of witches, but skinwalkers (most often male) are said to be the most powerful and deeply feared by the Navajo and Apache people.

Traditionally, skinwalkers are able to change themselves into dogs, and they wear the skin of a dog over their shoulders or the skull of a dog as a cap. So I guess that's the reason for the term. I've never had anyone explain it to me. It's something you don't talk about in polite company.

Hunt for the Skinwalker by Colm Kelleher and George Knapp is a book about a peculiar "taboo" ranch in Utah's Uinta Basin that is thought by some Utes to be "on the path of the skinwalker." A skinwalker doesn't necessarily have to be around to victimize you. He can come back later and gather magical samples to use to enact his willful agenda. Some Diné believe that skinwalkers can use the spit, hair and nail clippings to make curses. For this reason, many Navajo will never spit on the ground or even leave their shoes outside the door, and they take great care to see that any hair or nail clippings are burned or disposed of properly.

Knapp and Kelleher were told some interesting accounts by reservation law enforcement that have a similar feel to the aforementioned account. These nocturnal road encounters seem to make up a majority of skinwalker encounters by non-Native people.

One Caucasian family still speaks in hushed tones about its encounter with a skinwalker, even though it happened in 1983. While driving at night along Route 163 through the massive Navajo Reservation, the four members of the family felt that someone was following them. As their truck slowed down to round a sharp bend, the atmosphere changed, and time itself seemed to slow down. Then something leaped out of a roadside ditch at the vehicle.

"Whatever this thing was, it wore a man's clothes. It had on a white and blue checked shirt and long pants. Its arms were raised over its head, almost touching the top of the cab. It looked like a hairy man or a hairy animal in man's clothing, but it didn't look like an ape or anything like that. Its eyes were yellow and its mouth was open."

So, are skinwalkers lurking the canyons and arroyos of the 21st century haunted Southwest? Do they still force eye contact and absorb themselves into terrified victims and make them go places and do unspeakable things? Are they just a fading cultural myth that has amassed great and lasting power over superstitious people that still adhere to the belief that these black magicians are real and to be feared? Only the indigenous natives of the Southwestern United States can definitively answer this question by producing irrefutable evidence that these supernatural beings are indeed real. Thankfully, I've never encountered a skinwalker that has made its presence known in an unequivocal manner. Or have I?

Christopher O'Brien: Author, researcher and investigator in the fields of ufology, cryptids, and the paranormal.

FATE March-April 2011

Navajo Witchcraft
Sandra J. Wilson

My small son insisted that he had to go outside. It was after dark and my husband was out visiting a friend. I opened the door and started to step forward when I saw the tall, gray shape standing below me at the bottom of the steps. As I instinctively pushed my son backwards with my body, the shape sprang into the air, without stooping to gather itself, and sailed over the eight-foot fence.

For almost an hour we cowered in the house. The thing outside turned on the radio in the shade house and played with the volume. Finally, my husband pulled up in our noisy old truck. I threw the door open and shouted a warning. He chanted a Navajo protection prayer as we listened to the thing pounding swiftly across the desert.

The fear of witchcraft is alive and well on the Navajo reservation. Not only small children fear leaving their houses at night – adults who otherwise consider themselves quite modern still shudder at the hoot of an owl or the plaintive wail of a coyote too close to home.

I first learned of "skinwalkers," the practitioners of evil sorcery and shapeshifting, during my second year on the Navajo reservation. A year earlier, I had assisted in collecting videotaped testimony of Navajo families affected by Public Law 93-531, which required the relocation of thousands of Navajo and Hopi individuals. We collected these oral testimonies with the intent of producing a documentary on the so-called Navajo-Hopi Land Dispute under the direction of Professor David Hilligoss of Sangamon State University.

The following year I returned permanently to the reservation area to assist in the legal battle which resulted in Manybeads v. United States, which challenged federal right to relocate Navajo and Hopi Indians from their ancestral homes under the Relocation Act. It was during this effort that I won the friendship and trust of many of the people I worked with. And I joined the ranks of the uninitiated. It was common sport among the younger Navajo to tell skinwalker stories to the non-Indian activists and volunteers who came to work on the HPL.

Dark practices

Commonly called "witches," these individuals and their practice should not be confused with the Wiccan religion. Specifically, it is the *yiinaldloshi* who can transform him- or herself into an animal by donning its skin. The witch is said to perform a chant or ceremony which completes the transformation.

Coyotes, wolves and bears are common forms, and a *yiinal'* chooses a skin depending on the task he or she wishes to perform. A coyote might be chosen for speed, whereas a bear would be chosen for strength. An insect might be used to spy upon an intended victim.

But these dark practitioners are more than just werewolves. Each is involved in ceremonies designed to bring fear, sickness and death to their victims. They are grave robbers, who steal not only jewelry, but the flesh and bones of corpses that are transformed into "corpse powder" and bone beads. These beads are shot into intended victims, while corpse powder might be thrown down the smoke hole of a hogan or tossed onto a victim in a crowd, such as a sing or fair.

There are differing opinions as to whether a non-Indian can be affected by witchcraft. Some Navajo believe that nonIndians are completely immune. Others say that anyone is susceptible as long as they believe in the possibility.

Also in dispute is whether or not a *yiinaldloshi* can actually transmogrify into the shape of an animal. Either way, these practitioners are very real human beings, and as such have the capability of rendering great harm or death to another.

Indian traders, Indian agents and military personnel have played an important if controversial role in the history of the Southwest and Indian country in particular. Documented history reveals accounts of these parties being drawn into witchcraft-related incidents, whether they believed in the practice or not.

Army purges witches

The Navajo faced an infamous witch purge in 1878. This was 10 years after the treaty was signed between the United States and the Navajo people at Fort Sumner, which marked the end of Navajo imprisonment by the United States Army and the creation of a Navajo reservation.

Events leading up to the purge began three years after the release from Hweeldi, when a number of witches were captured and killed. In the fall of 1876, five witches were executed in the western portion of the reservation.

Charles Hubbell, brother of the better-known John Lorenzo Hubbell of Ganado, was employed by William B. Leonard to run the trading post at Ganado Lake. It was he who first notified Indian Agent John E. Pyle of events leading up to what would come to be known as the Witch Purge of 1878. In three items of correspondence, Hubbell related that a suspected witch had been killed, and that an uprising between Ganado and Canyon de Chelly Navajos was imminent.

Pyle passed this information on to Lt. Colonel P.T. Swain, in command of Fort Wingate. Swain dispatched two officers, 10 enlisted men and one civilian to protect the settlers of the region and attempt to pacify the Navajo.

Historians have suggested that the uprising was in fact political in nature, and the activities of a faction of Navajo opposed to the signing of the treaty posed a threat to other tribal leaders who supported the treaty, or at the very least recognized that cooperation with the federal government was necessary for the continued survival of the People. These men included famed headmen Ganado Mucho and Manuelito.

The accused leader of the anti-treaty faction was a man called Biwos or Biwosi. Biwosi was also suspected of being the leader of a band of witches. He was killed only a mile from the Hubbell Trading Post in Ganado before the military's arrival. Another suspected witch was killed in the doorway of the same trading post.

On June 10, Manuelito delivered a note to Ft. Wingate written by John Lorenzo Hubbell informing the military that six suspected witches had been detained and were facing execution. Lt. Mitchell and five enlisted men proceeded to the area then known as Navajo City, where Charles Hubbell and about 50 Navajos joined the party. Continuing to Tunicha Mountain Valley, the contingent found three Navajo bound and under guard. More people arrived as Mitchell ordered the men released, then ordered these suspected witches to desist in their practices. All three agreed readily. One of the men surrendered his medicine bundle to Mitchell.

The crowd was delighted with this performance and asked Mitchell to remain in the area so that they could bring in other suspected witches for a repeat performance. Four other men were to renounce the practice of witchcraft before Mitchell continued on to Ft. Defiance.

At least part of the witch bundle surrendered to Mitchell survives as evidence in the collection of the Medical Museum of the Armed Forces Institute of Pathology.

Charles Hubbell's involvement in the witch purge was not over. A man known as Haloishjohn came to Hubbell to ask for his assistance in investigating some possessions of several other Navajo that had been buried in the area. Haloishjohn and his companions were afraid to touch these items, and asked Hubbell to go dig them up.

In his personal account, he reported that these items, gathered by witches, had been wrapped in paper and stuffed into the abdomen of a corpse. He indicated that the paper appeared to be the Navajo copy of the Treaty of 1868.

This account added fuel to the belief that the anti-treaty party was involved in the incidents of this period.

Wetherill's bad luck

During the late 1930s, stock reduction programs became the fodder for many accusations of witchcraft Ben Wetherill, son of the archaeologist John Wetherill, was reservation-born and raised. He learned the Navajo language before English. His situation earned him the position of district supervisor over the Black Mesa area. That position, and his subsequent participation in the stock reduction effort, would place him in direct conflict with a witch known as Gani Choii.

One evening, after a difficult roundup of horses, an exhausted Wetherill collapsed into bed, only to be awakened later by his dogs. Dogs, it should be noted, are believed to have the ability to detect the presence of witches. Wetherill went outside to check on the gathered horses, and finding nothing wrong, returned to bed.

In the morning, he was to discover markings in the dirt outside his home which he recognized as evidence of witchcraft. He described in his writings a circle formed of white sand, marked with a small cross and an arrow aimed directly at his front door.

Wetherill called E. Ressman Fryer, the General Superintendent in Window Rock, who did not share Wetherill's belief in witchcraft. Fryer counseled the shaken man that a white man could not be witched, and that he should ignore the markings.

Despite this advice, further mishaps quickly occurred. One of the two mounted police under Wetherill was thrown from his horse and badly injured. The second policeman suffered a broken leg when his horse stepped into a prairie dog hole. A close friend lost two grandchildren, and Wetherill's marriage began a downhill spiral as his wife became increasingly restless and frightened.

Wetherill paid a visit to Fryer at Ft. Defiance when he brought his mounted officer to the hospital to have his leg set. He asked Fryer for an assignment off the Navajo reservation, but the General Supervisor managed to talk Wetherill into remaining at Black Mesa. On his return trip, the hapless Wetherill's truck rolled over.

Gani Choii, who was said to have caused the death of the grandchildren of Wetherill's friend, continued to bring death to the children of the area, and several medicine men complained to Fryer, stating that if the old witch remained in the area, he would be killed.

Wetherill was ordered to arrest Gani Choii, and he and several other men captured the old man and took him to Window Rock.

In a meeting between Fryer, Councilman Tom Claw, the mounted policemen and Wetherill, the old man confessed deeds and explained how he had performed the witching. But while he talked Gani Choii began to pick up small items which the onlookers feared could be against them, such as a burnt match and small bits of mud from the participant's shoes.

All but Fryer became anxious, and denounced the old witch's repentance. Gani Choii was thrown into protective custody to think things over. Two days later, the old witch once again announced that he would end his practice, and was taken to Pinon where he performed a prayer to reverse his previous witching. Afterwards, the Blessing Way was performed for Gani Choii by several medicine men, but all of this brought no comfort to Wetherill, who wrote that he had been unable to hear what the old man had sung. Despite the fact that Gani Choii had been able to handle a red-hot pitch knot from a fire as proof of his statement, Wetherill did not believe him.

He may have had just cause, for Wetherill's luck did not change. Even though he left the Pinon area to purchase a trading post between Gallup and Zuni, the move was too late to save his marriage. Later, he accidentally shot off the end of his foot, which led to amputation. His health declined and he became depressed. Until his untimely death, he blamed Gani Choii.

The murdered nurse

In 1986, the residents of Flagstaff, Arizona, were startled by the murder of Mary Saganitso, a nurse who worked at the Flagstaff Medical Center. Murder was and is a rare crime in this peaceful mountain town, and Mary's was the first in almost two decades. As the investigation continued, the fact that Mary had been raped and strangled would become the least important factor in the case.

Saganitso's mutilated body was found on a rocky slope behind the medical center, with one nipple having been bitten off. George William Abney, one-time professor of Northern Arizona University, also in Flagstaff, would later confess to the crime. Dental impressions taken from Abney satisfied the prosecution's expert that he was indeed the person who had bitten Saganitso.

The premier law firm of Aspey, Watkins and Diesel was hired to represent the confessed murderer. The defense would be a shocking one – the murder had actually been committed by a skinwalker.

From the pages of the Coconino County Superior Court case, expert witnesses included an Apache sweat lodge leader who worked with Navajo and a professor of folklore who had married a Navajo and who had lived on the reservation. A case for Abney's innocence developed.

Saganitso's body exhibited the removal of significant amounts of flesh and fatty tissue. There was also the presence of "grass" found near the site. A stick that had been carefully lain across the body was a key element in the defense. The fact that the wounds were crescent shaped was also taken into consideration.

There are those who believe that Abney was the actual murderer of the Navajo nurse. But the jury was persuaded that Saganitso was the victim of a skinwalker. Abney was acquitted.

Hitchhiking trickster

Since my relocation to the Upper Colorado Plateau, I have had many witchcraft related experiences. I will always remember my first benign meeting with a real comedian.

One summer evening in 1990, I was returning to Flagstaff from a visit to the Blue Canyon area of Tiicyatoh near Big Mountain. Relaxed and happy from a weekend among friends, I was nearing the reservation line, thinking of the chores I needed to perform before returning to work in the morning. Perhaps a mile ahead, a pick-up truck was suddenly punctuated by bright tail lights. The driver was dropping off a hitchhiker before heading up to a sheep camp. As I drew closer, I watched the young man step to the edge of the road. He was dangerously handsome, with long midnight hair flowing loose. His jeans jacket was unbuttoned, exposing a warm brown, muscular chest.

I signaled to pull off the road and waited for the man to run up to the car. The rear door opened and the car shifted under his weight as he settled in and shut the door. I looked over my left shoulder and signaled to pull back onto the roadway. Then, accelerating, I turned to ask my guest where he was going.

In the back seat of my little Firenza sat a wizened old man, short gray hair poking out from a greasy old baseball cap. He wore a long-sleeved flannel work shirt and sported the biggest toothless grin I'd seen in a long, long time.

A quick glance into the rearview mirror showed the open, empty expanse where a young warrior stood only moments before.

When I dropped the old trickster at the Diamond Corner Store, he was laughing out loud. Though I was not harmed, the experience changed my outlook on the world forever.

Witchcraft is indeed alive and well on the Navajo reservation – and non-Indians are not immune.

Sandra J. Wilson: Freelance journalist who lived and worked among the Navajo and Hopi.

FATE December 2001

So You Want to Be a Werewolf
Aaron Bennett

(Editor's note: The recipes and instructions in this article are taken from old folklore texts, and are not intended for use. They contain dangerous and poisonous materials.)

The following is a research paper for academic and educational use only. Do not attempt any of the activities mentioned herein. Severe bodily and/or mental harm may be incurred. The procurement of certain articles, plants, and herbs, as well as the enactment of the pertaining rites, may be considered unlawful in certain areas. You may be subject to legal penalties and imprisonment. Check with local authorities before attempting any such rite as outlined below. The writer and publisher assume no responsibility for persons attempting to perform the acts set forth in this article. The author disavows any statement about harming or killing animals.

Preparations

I have pieced together the following rite from many different manuscripts and old books. First off, a person wanting to become a werewolf must pick a powerful night to enact the ceremony. Walpurgis Night was often chosen as a night very conducive to shifting into a werewolf. This night is made even more special since Saint Walburga (A.O. 710-779), for whom the day is named, is the patron saint of werewolves. This night falls on May Day Eve. Some other nights to try this rite would be Samhain (Halloween), the night of a lunar eclipse, or even just a full moon.

The operator must first construct a belt or girdle made from a strip of wolf hide. This strip has to be at least three fingers wide. It must have a buckle with seven tangs or seven tongues. In the middle of the back, five iron nail heads are affixed into a pattern forming the points of a pentagram. Nails that have been galvanized (treated with zinc) should be avoided. This may adversely affect the power of the girdle. While constructing this belt, the would-be werewolf must say the following:

> *On the sea, on the ocean, on the island, on Bujan,*
> *On the empty pasture gleams the moon, on an ashstock lying*
> *In a green wood, in a gloomy vale.*
> *Toward the stock wand ereth a shaggy wolf,*
> *Horned cattle seeking for his sharp white fangs;*
> *But the wolf enters not the forest,*
> *But the wolf dives not into the shadowy vale,*
> *Moon, moon, gold-horned moon,*
> *Check the flights of bullets, blunt the hunter's knives,*
> *Break the shepherd's cudgels,*
> *Cast wild fear upon all cattle,*
> *On men, on all creeping things,*
> *That they may not catch the gray wolf,*
> *That they may not rend his warm skin!*
> *My word is binding, more binding than sleep,*
> *More binding than the promise of a hero!*

(Sabine Baring-Gould, *The Book of Werewolves*)

Then make the following formal declaration:

I [insert name here] offer to thee, Great Spirit of the Unknown, this night [insert date here], my body and soul, on condition that thou grantest me, from this night to the hour of my death, the power of metamorphosing, nocturnally, into a wolf. I beg, I pray, I implore thee, unparalleled Phantom of Darkness – to make me a werewolf.. .a werewolf!

(Quoted in Ian Woodward, *The Werewolf Delusion*, New York: Paddington Press, 1979)

'Tis Night

The hopeful werewolf must then obtain some pure spring water for use in the ceremony. This should be done at night, under the moon. If at all possible, the water should be carried in an iron vessel. While procuring the water, the following incantation must be said:

'Tis night! 'tis night! and the moon shines white
Over pine and snow-capped hill;
The shadows stray through burn and brae
And dance in the sparkling rill.
'Tis night! 'tis night! and the Devil's light
Casts glimmering beams around.
The maras dance, the nisses prance
On the flower-enameled ground.
'Tis night! 'tis night! and the werewolf's might
Makes man and nature shiver.
Yet its fierce gray head and stealthy tread
Are naught to thee, oh river!
River, river, river.
Oh water strong, that swirls along,
I prithee a werewolf make me.
Of all the things dear, my soul, I swear,
In death shall not forsake thee.

(Quoted by Woodward)

The operator must find a suitable spot to perform the ceremony. This should be a desolate place away from any possible human interference, such as a clearing in a forest, a mountaintop, a desert, or even an abandoned parking lot, although this last one might present some trouble. It is necessary that the bladder be emptied immediately before commencing the ceremony to cleanse the body of the human toxins that might inhibit the transformation concoctions.

The circle
A circle with a radius of more than seven feet, but less than nine feet, is marked off with string, chalk, or pitch (tar). Another circle with a radius of three feet is placed in the center of the larger circle. In this smaller circle, a fire is constructed. The fire may be made out of black poplar, pine, or larch (Larix europaea). Under no circumstances must ash wood be used, as it will actually inhibit the process. An iron pot is placed in a tripod above the fire. The spring water is poured into the pot, as well as a concoction of four or five of the following:

> Hemlock (Conium maculatum) – two to three ounces
> Henbane (Hyoscyamus niger) – one ounce to an ounce
>   and a half
> Saffron (Crocus sativa) – three ounces
> Poppy Seed (Papaver spp.) – any amount
> Aloe (Aloe vera) – three drachms
> Opium (Papaver somniferum) – one-quarter ounce
> Asafoetida or Devil's Dung (Ferula foetida) – two ounces
> Solanum or Black Nightshade (Solanum dulcamara) –
>   two to three drachms
> Parsley (Petroselinum sativum) – any amount

> (From Elliot O'Donnell, *Werewolves*, London: Methuen, 1912)

In modern measurements, one drachm equals eight ounces.
Notice that most of the ingredients are poisonous. Ingestion of any of these will result in great bodily harm or even death.

More chanting

This mixture is then brought to a boil while chanting the following verses (also quoted by O'Donnell):

> *Spirits from the deep*
> *Who never sleep,*
> *Be kind to me.*
> *Spirits from the grave*
> *Without a soul to save,*
> *Be kind to me.*
> *Spirits of the trees*
> *That grow upon the leas,*
> *Be kind to me.*
> *Spirits of the air,*
> *Foul and black, not fair,*
> *Be kind to me.*
> *Water spirits hateful,*
> *To ships and bathers fateful,*
> *Be kind to me.*
> *Spirits of the earthbound dead*
> *That glide with noiseless tread,*
> *Be kind to me.*
> *Spirits of heat and fire,*
> *Destructive in your ire,*
> *Be kind to me.*
> *Spirits of cold and ice,*
> *Patrons of crime and vice,*
> *Be kind to me.*
> *Wolves, vampires, satyrs, ghosts!*
> *Elect of all the devilish hosts!*
> *I pray you send hither,*
> *Send hither, send hither,*
> *The great gray shape that makes men shiver!*
> *Shiver, shiver, shiver!*
> *Come! Come! Come!*

The operator then removes all clothing. A salve is subsequently applied to the body consisting of, to begin with, the fat from some newly killed animal, preferably a baby animal or a cat. Into this is mixed aniseed (*Pimpinella anisum*), camphor (*Cinnamomum camphora*), and opium.

The girdle

The operator then places the girdle around the waist and fastens all of the buckles or straps. While doing this, the following incantation is recited.

> *Hail, hail, hail, great wolf spirit, hail!*
> *A boon I ask thee, mighty shade.*
> *Within this circle I have made,*
> *Make me a werewolf strong and bold*
> *The terror alike of young and old.*
> *Grant me a figure tall and spare;*
> *The speed of an elk, the claws of a bear*
> *The poison of snakes, the w it of a fox*
> *The stealth of a wolf, the strength an ox;*
> *The jaws of a tiger, the teeth of a shark*
> *The eyes of a cat that sees in the dark*
> *Make me climb like a monkey, scent like a dog,*
> *Swim like a fish, and eat like a hog.*
> *Haste, haste, haste, lonely spirit, haste!*
> *Here, wan and drear, magic spell making,*
> *Findest thou me shaking, quaking,*
> *Softly fan me as I lie,*
> *And thy mystic touch apply*
> *Touch apply, and swear that when I die,*
> *When I die, I will serve thee evermore,*
> *Evermore, in grey wolf land, cold and raw.*

The operator then kisses the ground three times, walks slowly to the fire and picks up the iron pot, lifts the pot aloft, and whirls around counterclockwise. While doing this, the following incantation is spoken, loudly:

> *Make me a werewolf! Make me a man-eater!*
> *Make me a werewolf! Make me a woman-eater!*

Make me a werewolf! Make me a child-eater!
I pine for blood! Human blood! Give it to me! Give it me
tonight! Great Wolf Spirit! Give it me, and Heart, body,
and soul, I am yours.

The spirit comes

Then the werewolf hopeful kneels inside the small circle and waits for the spirit to come and grant the request. The operator must sit and wait for the fire to burn blue or rise up suddenly for no apparent reason. If the experiment worked, the spirit will come and touch the person, granting his or her request.

This spirit will only appear long enough to touch the individual. It comes and goes in complete silence. Descriptions of this spirit vary widely in various accounts. It could be possible that the spirit appears differently to each person according to what the person thinks that the spirit should look like. It could even come in the form of an amorphous blob that has no discernable shape. No matter what the spirit looks like, the important part is that it grants the person's request to become a werewolf. This instilling of the power to metamorphose is the all-important event and the culmination of this ceremony. Once a person has this power, he may shift anytime he wants. It may be required to wear the girdle and reapply the salve, but the power should not leave the person unless he is exorcised of it.

To rid himself of the wolf shape, the operator must immerse himself in cool, running water. Then the girdle is removed. The girdle must be hidden somewhere where no one will be able to discover it. Who knows what evil can come from putting the power of transformation in the wrong hands!

Gathering materials

Procurement of articles for this ritual is a daunting task in itself. A strip of wolf's hide may be obtained from a taxidermist or a furrier. I suggest checking out firms in Alaska and upper Canada, as wolf skins are more readily available in these areas. That also means they might be obtained for less money, which is always good. In a pinch, a coyote hide might do the trick. These are much more widely available and are much cheaper. One should check with his local post office as to the legality of getting a wolf hide shipped to him.

Please be advised that wolves are an endangered species in most regions of the United States. Killing one could result in hefty fines and imprisonment. I personally would like to see the wolves come back. I do not agree with the senseless killing of these beautiful creatures, especially for some magical ceremony.

Some of the herbs are widely available. Saffron and poppy seeds may be found in the spice section of any grocery store. Parsley is used the world over. One should be able to find some in any produce section, or dried in the spice section. Anise is pretty much the same. American fennel may also be used if the European kind is not available. There is also a liqueur made from the anise plant called anisette that could be used. Aloe is widely available in any store that sells indoor plants. The pure aloe vera can be purchased in a drug store. It is really useful for sun and other types of burns. Camphor oil may also be purchased in any good pharmacy or drug store.

Most of the other herbs mentioned can be purchased through a Wiccan supply store or an herbalist.

The operator is on his own for the opium, a controlled substance. *Let me reiterate that many of these ingredients, especially the ones not readily available, are poisonous and/or dangerous. Using them in any manner will result in physical harm or even death! Use at your own risk.*

Danger of rabies

There are plenty of other theories and legends pertaining to becoming a werewolf. This is just one that I chose to explore. I dismiss many of the stories that entail biting or scratching as a method to gain the werewolf "curse." I believe that most of these legends stem from what we now know as rabies, the symptoms of which closely parallel eyewitness accounts of possessed persons thinking themselves to be werewolves. This can especially be seen in the trial accounts from the Middle Ages. I believe that the method that involves drinking rainwater from a wolf's paw print and drinking from a pool that three or more wolves have bathed in is linked to rabies as well. A dog will spend countless hours licking his or her paws. Rabies may be left on the paw and hence transferred to the paw print. A small pool might contain enough of the rabies virus if many infected wolves frequented it. As a series of rabies shots is a very painful process, I do not recommend anyone attempt these methods in order to become a "werewolf." If left untreated, rabies will lead to an even more painful death.

Aaron Bennett: Freelance writer and English teacher.

FATE July 2002

SPECTRAL AND DEMON DOGS

THE HOUNDS OF HELL
Kelly Bell

The people of Bungay, Suffolk, in England gave little thought to the lowering skies as they assembled for worship services on Sunday, August 4, 1577. Thunderstorms are commonplace in the dreary British Isles, but this tempest was preceded by a midnight type darkness. As a violent gale swept through the church, ripping shutters from their hinges, the fearful parishioners realized something untoward had joined the services.

Illuminated by flashes of lightning, a monstrous form galloped howling among the congregation. It looked to the Godfearing churchgoers like a bigger than usual floppy-eared Pyrenees sheep dog except that it was tar black. Terrified by this fearsome apparition, most of the witnesses dropped to their knees in prayer. The specter passed between two of these praying supplicants, brushing against them and striking both dead. One onlooker later described how a third man the creature grazed "shriveled up like a drawn purse," but survived.

After a few more seconds of rushing among the panicked church members, the yowling vision charged out the building's north door. To this day cryptic burn marks left by the phantom remain visible on the wooden door. The metal workings of the church's belfry clock were left twisted and broken by the creature's passing.

Later that morning the same or a similar demon visited another church seven miles away and wrought similar havoc. Survivors described how it killed two men and "blasted" everyone else.

Satanic canines

Everyone knows of the standard animal familiars of the unholy. Black cats, pigs, goats, bats, and snakes have been associated with Satan since the Garden of Eden. Halloween would not be complete without them. Yet perhaps the most terrifying animal form assumed by the Lord of Darkness and his minions has remained mysteriously obscure. Although dogs were so revered by followers of the Egyptian goddess Isis that her worshippers feasted on dog meat, perhaps being man's best friend has shielded the humble, lovable dog from earning a reputation that by all rights should have ruined its wholesome image.

The Suffolk monsters were not isolated cases, nor were they anything new. In fact, the people of this region had had so many encounters with hellish black dogs that by the time of the 1577 incidents they had hung the nickname "Old Shock" on the phantom. Similar creatures had become well established throughout the United Kingdom by this period. Somerset had its "Gurt Dog," and Ireland was haunted by "Pooka."

During the 1980s outbreaks of livestock killing in England were pinned by some investigators on a huge black dog. In 1982 the situation had progressed to the point that the military was sent to track down the cattle ripper, which by then had killed almost 100 sheep around the city of Stokenchurch. The Royal Marines were unable to get close enough to bag the beast, but many of them saw it and claimed it resembled a giant dog.

A ghostly dog haunted the area around Tring in Hartford throughout the 19th century. Local lore held that a woman who was drowned there as a witch in 1751 returned in canine form. One undated account from the local Book of Days contains this anonymous report:

I was returning home late one night in a gig with the person who was driving. When we came near the spot where a portion of the gibbet had lately stood we saw on the bank of the roadside a flame of fire as large as a man's hat. 'What's that?' I exclaimed. 'Hush!' said my companion, and suddenly pulling in his horse, came to a dead stop. I then saw an immense black dog just in front of our horse, the strangest looking creature I ever beheld. He was as big as a Newfoundland, but very gaunt, shaggy, with long ears and tail, eyes like balls of fire, and large, long teeth, for he opened his mouth and seemed to grin at us. In a few minutes the dog disappeared, seeming to vanish like a shadow or to sink into the earth, and we drove over the spot where he had lain.

Blood drinking sheep killers

In 1810 something was killing sheep and cattle along the border between England and Scotland. The predator would rip out animals' throats and drink the blood as it gushed out. It killed eight to ten head of stock per night.

These killings abruptly stopped in September when a posse of farmers shot a dog and burned its body. This solitary vampire dog must have had a prodigious thirst to have drained eight to ten sheep and cows of their blood nightly.

In early 1874 something was killing as many as 30 sheep per night around Cavan, Ireland, and consuming nothing but their blood. Other than gaping throats, the anemic carcasses were untouched. Armed farmers took to the fields to protect their livelihood. They found nothing but peculiar tracks that looked canine, but much larger than any known dog's and strangely elongated. By the end of the year the killings had dwindled away to nothing and the case was never solved.

It is an established fact that outbreaks of this sort are characterized by sudden, unpredictable appearances of mystery canines that wreak a great deal of bloody havoc, throw large geographic areas into turmoil, then disappear without a trace upon the advent of serious investigation, usually never to return. This mystery within a mystery is as resistant to being solved as is the overall phenomenon, and hints at a complex occult connection.

Perhaps outbreaks of paranormal canines should not he too surprising coming from ghost-loving Britain. These mysterious islands have traditionally bred reams of tales of the unexplained, and are renowned as the most haunted part of the globe. Yet reports of otherworldly dogs are well distributed throughout time and place.

In A.D. 856, what an account in the *Annales Francorum Regum* called "a dog of immense size" violated a Christian church in Trier, Prussia. Once again, a violent electrical storm was in progress and members of the congregation were sitting in almost total darkness when the beast seemed to rise through the unbroken floor and for several minutes rushed back and forth along the center aisle from the front door to the altar before disappearing.

Demonic terriers

During the 7th century, the Middle East was periodically bedeviled by what old records call "a plague of frightening and terrible animals" that sound vaguely like demonic rat terriers with bristly fins on their backs. The ancient *Chronicon of Denys de Tell-Mahre* describes them thusly: "Their muzzle was small and long, and they had great ears like those of horses. The skin on their dorsal spine resembled the bristles of pigs and stood straight up."

Ranging over a huge area of Armenia and Assyria, these terrors carried off children and whole flocks of sheep and goats, while killing many men who tried to fight them. For some reason dogs would not bark at the creatures, and when they raided villages at night the inhabitants would not know they were under attack until it was too late. It seemed there was little to be done to resist the beasts anyway. After despoiling hundreds of square miles for an undetermined period, they disappeared forever.

In 1893 a creature described as long and black with a blunt muzzle, long tail, and round, erect ears terrorized the district around Orel, Russia, killing a number of women and children. Although it seems to have resembled a black lioness, it left behind enormous doglike tracks. After a short reign of terror, it too simply vanished.

Oversized dog tracks have a habit of turning up in areas of heavy paranormal activity. Occult investigator John Keel found them during his investigation of the creepy goings-on around and over Point Pleasant, West Virginia, in 1967-68. His research in this locality resulted in his blockbuster book *The Mothman Prophecies*, which one would think might have propelled the cryptic canine connection to the arcane into greater prominence. Yet this mystical element continues to elude widespread notice.

Still, there are those who have taken note of the evil that sometimes seems to emanate from the trustworthy, loving, and loyal dog. As recently as 1975 an unnamed elderly man and his four adult sons in Varasdin, Croatia were arrested for trying to burn at the stake an old woman they accused of having attacked them in the guise of a huge black dog with fiery eyes. They had tied their victim to a stake, piled straw around her and were in the act of lighting the fire when horrified townspeople interrupted the execution.

There is no record of whether the old woman was innocent, or, if not, how many more like her might there be.

Kelly Bell: Freelance writer concentrating on military history and the esoteric.

FATE November 2006

BLACK DOGS: FACT OR FANCY
Gordon Stein

Of course, black dogs exist. My neighbor even has one. So, what do I mean about whether black dogs are fact or fancy? These are a very special type of black dog, namely the ones that seem to appear suddenly alongside you on a dark country road, run along with you for a while, and then vanish suddenly. Usually, they are harmless, even if scary. However, they sometimes have been reported to be quite nasty and evil.

Church worshippers attacked by black dogs

For example, on a Sunday morning in August 1577, the people at the church in the British town of Bungay had quite a shock. In the middle of the service, a severe storm arose outside. Suddenly, a large black dog appeared in the middle of the church. He ran between two members of the congregation who were kneeling in prayer. The dog evidently "wrung the necks of them bothe in one instant clene backward, insomuch that even at a moment where they kneeled, they strangely dyed."

In this case, another worshipper was bitten by the dog on the back. The bite caused the man to be "presently drawen togither and shrunk up, as if [he] were a piece of lether scorched in a hot fire ... "The man "dyed not, but it is thought is yet alive."

A similar incident involving a black dog in church happened that same month (some accounts say that same day) in another church at Blythburgh, about seven miles away. In the latter incident, the dog appeared on a beam in the church, swung down and "slew two men and a lad, and burned the hand of another person that was there among the rest of the company, of whom divers were blasted." There was supposedly a set of burn marks left on the church door by the dog as he left.

Hundreds of years later, the paint was scraped from the doors of this church by workmen, revealing the presence of what appear to be scorch marks.

Of course, this type of attack by a black dog is no longer anything that has been reported. Yes, some of the dogs have been reported to snarl menacingly and not let you pass, but the attacks and deaths are a thing of the past. The black dog is often still thought of as a sign from the devil, but at least the devil isn't using the dogs to kill.

Are black dogs real?

Some say that these black dog "sightings" are real historical events. The people who say they saw black dogs of a spectral sort really *did* see them, although the "dogs" were clearly of a supernatural sort.

Another school of thought says that the people who claim sightings may well *believe* that they saw a mysterious black dog, but whatever it was that served as the focus of the sighting – the idea or image of the black dog – was something from deep inside the viewer's mind. To this school of thought the black dog is a symbolic image of evil, something that black dogs have represented to humanity for thousands of years.

This is the old conflict between the historian and the folklorist. The historian wants to know what *really* happened. The folklorist simply cares what people *believed*. I will adopt the position of the folklorist in this article.

There is, of course, no way for us to decide at this point whether any of these incidents really happened. If someone with a movie or videotape camera were to photograph or film the supposed black dog during a sighting, and the film or tape showed nothing when viewed, then perhaps the folklorist might feel vindicated for accepting what people believed. If, however, an image of a black dog appeared on the film or videotape, exactly as reported, then the first explanation might be more likely. Unfortunately, no photographic evidence exists for any black dog sighting.

There is at least one additional complication to this set of two possibilities. It is also possible that a layer of myth (perhaps in part derived from fictional treatments of the black dog theme, as in Goethe's *Faust*), is superimposed upon some actual historical cases. This happens in many other fields, such as with UFOs. There are quite a few fictional accounts of UFO encounters that have been passed off as real. Exactly how many such "real" cases remain after the probable fictitious ones are removed is an open question, both for UFOs and for black dogs.

Sightings of black dogs

The interesting thing about the black dog is how widely it has been reported in the United Kingdom. The Germans have also reported seeing it. However, France and the United States don't seem to be among its favorite areas. There are very few reports of mysterious black dogs in the United States, but the U.S. seems to specialize in mysterious humans and humanoids.

This richness of British sightings is probably due to the fact that there is a long tradition of such sightings in Britain. Therefore, folklorists are more likely to record and investigate reports of black dogs than would other agencies (e.g., the police) in other countries. There would be little likelihood of police involvement in any case, since none of the more modem reports I can identify involves any real harm to the humans involved. Even in the United Kingdom, the types of reports and name given to the mysterious dog(s) varies.

Among the names given to this phenomenon (and hence to the dog itself) are Shuck (Black Shuck and Old Shuck as well), Skeff, Moddey Dhoo, Trash, Skriker, Padfoot, Hooter and Gwyllgi. This wide variety of names gives us the additional information that the sightings have been widespread, both geographically and in time.

Black Shuck.

What do the sightings have in common? Most of the dogs are seen at night, have glowing red eyes, vanish when you attempt to touch them, are silent, non-hostile, and leave no footprints, even in the mud. There are numerous exceptions to each one of these characteristics in many reports.

These sightings did not only take place in the past. Theo Brown, perhaps the leading British authority on the subject, identified some 39 incidents in Britain from 1829 to 1958, when her paper on this subject was published.

Scratching noises

At the edge of Dartmoor in southern England in 1972, a farmer and his wife were awakened by scratching noises outside their bedroom door. The farmer got out of bed and looked outside the bedroom door into the hall. He could see little at first, but when he reached the top of the stairs, he saw a large shadow. It appeared to be a dog. Just as he was about to shoo it outside with the poker he was carrying for protection, the dog moved toward him. Its eyes were fiery red. The farmer struck out at it. As he hit it, there was a burst of light, the crash of breaking glass, and the dog vanished completely. Later, the farmer and his wife discovered several interesting things as they examined their home. The electricity was out in the entire house, and every window was broken. There were broken roof tiles all over the outside yard. The roofs of a number of neighborhood houses had also been badly damaged.

The earliest incident involving a black dog of which we have a record seems to be from a French account by Bertin in the *Annales Franorum Regnum*, written in 856 A.D. About halfway through the services in a small French village church, darkness enveloped the building. A large, black dog mysteriously appeared inside the church, its eyes glowing fiercely. The animal ran around the inside of the church, as if looking for something. It then suddenly disappeared without a trace.

Harbinger of death?

On the Isle of Man in 1927, a black dog was encountered by a man on a road near Ramsey. The dog blocked the road and refused to let the man pass. After this blockade went on for a short time, the dog moved aside and let the man pass. Shortly thereafter the father of the man died.

The interpretation was that the dog had brought the message of the impending death. Black dogs have often been called harbingers of death.

Another example of this premonition of death can be seen in a 1893 Norfolk, England case. Two men driving a horse cart were forced to stop the cart suddenly due to the appearance of a black dog in the middle of the road. The driver wanted to drive straight at the dog; the passenger urged him against it. Finally, the driver's patience ran out, and he whipped the horse forward. As the cart touched the dog, there was the smell of sulfur, and the dog vanished in a ball of flame. Within a few days, the driver died unexpectedly.

Phantom dogs and the church

Many British rural people thought that black dogs were "church grimes." These are a sort of spirit that guards church-yards (i.e., small church cemeteries) from the devil. The origins of this belief may be traced to the old practice of burying a black dog (of the ordinary sort) on the north side of the church cemetery, in order to spare a human soul from having to guard the graveyard. It was thought that this duty fell to the first person buried in the churchyard. This early affiliation of churches and black dogs may help to explain why many of the early sightings were in the vicinity of churches.

Interestingly, many reports of phantom dogs state that the dog appeared unaware of the human being who saw it. The dog apparently "haunted" a section of road or an area. Sometimes the black dogs seem to be on patrol in an area. Often bridges mark the beginning or end of a phantom dog's patrol spot.

Black dogs and ley lines

Some writers who investigate black dogs (e.g., Janet and Colin Bord) feel that the locations of sightings can be linked with leys. Ley theory says that many ancient sites were located along straight lines from each other. These lines are called leys and represented some sort of earth current or energy flow pattern. Perhaps, the Bords state, black dog "patrols" occur along these leys. Many churches (and their churchyards) were built upon the sites of earlier pagan shrines, the location of which, in turn, was often on a ley line. The Bords even hypothesize that the appearance of black dogs themselves may be due to a "current" passing along the leys. Since the presence of such a current has never actually been demonstrated, their idea is pure speculation.

Black dogs battle real dogs

What happens when a ghostly black dog meets a real live dog? Actually, there are several occasions when this happened, all of which indicates that there is some physical reality to ghostly black dogs. Pierre van Passen (in 1939) tells what happened when he allowed his two police dogs to meet a ghostly black dog that passed his house regularly. The dogs (who were inside) leaped for the door. They bared their fangs and snarled. They howled as if they were in pain. Although the black dog could not be seen this time by the human, the dogs reportedly snapped and bit in all directions. The battle lasted two minutes. Then one of the "real" dogs fell on the floor and died.

The appearance of black dogs has sometimes been ended by the performance of an exorcism ritual, or by the display of religious artifacts. It is difficult to know what to make of this, as there have been very few such cases.

Devils and black dogs

In folklore from continental Europe, there are instances of the devil appearing in the form of a dog (often a black dog). This tradition does not seem to mean that all (or even most) black dog sightings (especially not the British sightings, where there is no such tradition), are an appearance by the devil. Although some devil appearances may be in the form of a black dog, the reverse is not true. Phantom dogs have also been said to occasionally guard treasures.

What is the explanation for black dogs?

Phantom dogs are something that few people have tried to explain. Theo Brown has made a couple of attempts, but I will leave it to the reader to judge how successful they have been.

She feels that one possibility is that the black dog is an aspect of a person at every stage of life, in a Jungian sense. They are projections from the unconscious, manifesting themselves visually at times of crisis. It could be viewed as a sort of "friendly double" in disguise. Going against this interpretation most strongly is the fact that black dogs have appeared to different people at the same spot. It is the location and not the person that seems to matter.

Another possible "explanation" offered by Brown is that it is probably impossible to explain the black dog in its own terms. By that she means that the more we think of the black dog as a *phenomenon*, the more difficult it is to explain. If, however, we could find some ancient cult or sect that had dogs as a symbol or "totem," perhaps we could compare our black dogs with them for significance. The lack of such evidence from history indicates that the symbolism aspect of black dogs is what is important.

Some aspects of dog mythology that are based upon real-dog behavior may be of help. A dog howls at the moon, similar to a wolf. It can be an intimate associate of humans (a possible symbol for a vampire-like creature). It protects property (i.e., it has a guardian function). It scavenges, and thus it is associated with death and graveyards. It sees "spirits," and so may serve as a link between this world and the next.

The one thing which does seem clear is that the black dog of British folklore seems to live outside of the concept of human time. It appears and disappears from human sight by its own contrivance.

Conclusion

What are we to make of all of this? Frankly, I don't know. We can hold all black dog stories up to the standard demanded by the historian, and then dismiss them as lacking sufficient evidence. We can also treat them (as I would prefer) as evidence of some sort of experienced perception on the part of the viewer. How we are to *interpret* this perception is another matter. Perhaps all black dog perceptions originate in the mind of the *observer*. That doesn't make the black dog phenomenon any less worthy of investigation and explanation. Right now, we are still back in the data-gathering stage. Any real explanation will have to await more data.

Gordon Stein (1941-96): Author and activist for atheism and religious skepticism.

FATE June 1990

BLACK MAGIC
Trevor Beer

Hail to the fearsome Black Hounds of English myth and legend. Long may they haunt – and help – us.

Many a writer has written of ghost hounds and the like, but among these apparitions the name Black Shuck is perhaps the best known – and treated with the most respect.

Black Shuck of East Anglia haunts wild Norfolk, England. A huge black dog with glowing red eyes, Black Shuck has been around for over a thousand years. He is a wonderful creature, an awesome spirit, and he bears a name which is itself a variation the Saxon word for the Devil.

Stand in the wilds of Norfolk on a stormy night when the wind howls – snatching at one's clothes – as the seas are tossed onto the mainland roads and sand dunes. At such times, it is difficult to stand upright. Such are the forces of nature – the very same that bring the howling spectral hound that is Black Shuck.

Black Shuck, by Trevor Beer.

The light from nearby inn windows and the knowledge that all is well within, makes it worse somehow for those of us foolhardy enough to explore Black Shuck's domain. For in these wild and windy haunts, the tides race in at terrifying speed, filling the black creek arms of marshes at such a rate that, suddenly silver lit and treacherous, they reach out for the unwary traveler.

But here too is magic. To not savor such moments, nor have such memories is almost folly itself for those of us steeped in the ways of folklore and legend.

As a young man, I stood at such a place near Cromer on a night when a howling wind allowed only glimpses of a moon hidden by sheets of black rain clouds.

Thank God at such times for an onshore wind! At least to be blown inland is security of a kind. I have crouched to the ground in gales on the North Devonshire coast, clutching at the grass and gorse bushes, afraid I might be blown to sea.

At Cromer, I did not see Black Shuck myself. I felt disappointed afterwards. Who can say how I would have felt had I seen him? Courage in hindsight comes easy.

But is Black Shuck really such a bad creature of the Devil? Certainly, where he is lord over his domain, he does provide ominous news that some life may be at stake out at sea. After all, he is a creature of the storms and a spectre of the sea coast more than inland, where he often roams headless near Coltishall and Norwich.

Well, then, is this dark beast a carrier of ominous tidings? But is Black Shuck not also serving the purpose of warning those abroad at such times? His very presence speaks of worsening storms and dangerous times ahead.

Why do locals not take the cliff paths in these horrid weather conditions? For fear of meeting Black Shuck! For by heeding the signs and fearing the consequences, we remain on safer ground. Not such a bad thing... Indeed, we must toss him a spectral dog biscuit next time he's about - and so it is, too, with the notorious Black Dog of Devon, and other dark canines of the night.

Long may they haunt our highways and byways.

Trevor Beer: Practicing naturalist, author, wildlife artist, and researcher of cryptozoology, dowsing, and folklore.

FATE July 1999

RETURN TO BLACK DOGS
Mark Chorvinsky

"Black Dog" cases are not simply a part of folklore, but have continued to occur in modern times. My research and investigation has shown that, if anything, the cases are more pervasive than researchers have thought.

One such case came to my attention last Halloween when I was a guest on a radio talk show. A caller, Frederick Deare, 42, of Baltimore, Maryland, had a memorable Black Dog encounter when he was 11 or 12 years old. I contacted Mr. Deare after the show and interviewed him at length. I consider him to be a highly credible witness (despite his age at the time of the event) who clearly remembers his strange encounter and has no doubt about the reality of the event.

The case occurred around 1959-1960 in Mr. Deare's boyhood home at 804 South Sharpe St. in South Baltimore. It was a snowy night in Baltimore and only two people were still awake in the Deare household – Frederick and his mother. Frederick was watching television and his mother was reading a novel in another room. The young man sensed that there was something outside the house. Frederick had a strong feeling that he was being watched. (This "feeling of being watched" is a very common element in all sorts of strange encounter cases.)

A huge head with strange eyes

Frederick looked out of the window and was shocked to see a huge head peering in at him. He looked closer – the thing outside his window was a huge, black dog.

The size of it, particularly the head, stunned Frederick. The dog must have been truly gigantic because it was standing on all fours. It had neither of its front paws on the waist-high window, yet its head was not only window height, but was actually lowered somewhat.

Frederick just sat there, shocked. The huge-headed animal was looking at him. He remembers that the dog's large eyes were "not normal animal eyes." The eyes were not round but slightly oval. The eyes were very large, even for a dog of this size. While Frederick can't recall specifically, he remembers that the eyes were either bright red or yellowish.

He called to his mother to look out the window. She did, also seeing the tremendous animal with the strange eyes. She dropped her book to the floor and told Frederick to walk toward her. The two of them went upstairs and shut and locked the doors. When Frederick glanced out of the upstairs window, the creature was nowhere to be seen.

Phantom dog leaves no tracks

Shortly thereafter he went outside. Although it was snowing there were no tracks anywhere outside the house. It had not snowed enough to cover up any fresh tracks. Mrs. Deare told Frederick that she had seen the creature but later tried to sweep the incident under the rug. Frederick had never heard of a creature like this before his sighting, and was not aware of other "Black Dog" cases until he heard me speak on the radio.

It may be important to note that Deare describes the house where the Black Dog appeared as "not your average house." From the time that his grandmother had moved there from Richmond, Virginia, there had been tales of strange happenings around the house. Most of its occupants had something strange happen to them, many hearing odd noises. It was said that grisly murders had occurred in the house and was common knowledge that someone had been killed on the second floor. On the third floor a man was either hanged or hanged himself.

After Frederick Deare's family moved from the house, realtors, for some reason, could not sell it. Recently, Mr. Deare visited his boyhood home. Although most of South Baltimore has been torn down and rebuilt – including the lots surrounding his old home – on the one lot where his house had stood nothing has been built.

Imported black-dog like entity?

Leslie Merette (also of Baltimore, Maryland) wrote to me about a series of Black Dog-related incidents that were really affecting her life. I interviewed her at length. Her case is quite different from the "average" Black Dog encounter, but there are similarities. One of the major differences in her case is that Leslie has placed her experiences into a frame of reference based on her interest in metaphysical subjects.

Ms. Merette believes that she originally "picked up" the Black Dog in the Dominican Republic – where she lived for seven years – and brought it to Baltimore with her. "A peculiar characteristic of this one is [that] it can manifest as a dog or as a man with a dog mask. When it comes as a dog it is a huge, full-formed black dog. This being has also been seen by friends of mine around me," she says.

Leslie believes that the dogbeing is persecuting her. "There has been a war going on. Well, it's continued. This beast – this black dog – the last time it appeared to me I was in Connecticut on a trip and it came to my motel room and tried to get in the door and was howling and scratching outside the door. On that trip, I found a statue from the Ivory Coast of a witch doctor with a dog's head mask that you can take off and put on. It's just been a theme in my life for the last nine years." The Black Dog/dog-man has appeared in Leslie's paintings as well. I asked Leslie if she thought the creature was a subjective· or objective phenomenon. Could it, for example, have been an archetypal image?

"It's real"

Leslie answered, "It's real. There's no question in my mind. It's not only real, it's been following me around. I thought at some point that it was a Jungian projection, but it isn't."

Leslie thought that it might have been subjective until her friend, Julie, also saw it in Leslie's room when they were in Vieques, a little island off the eastern coast of Puerto Rico. (I have not interviewed Julie at this time, but hope to in the future.)

"She didn't even tell me it was happening at first," Leslie recalls. "She thought it was too weird and kept silent about it. Later on in the trip she started telling me about it and I went, 'Whoa, wait a minute. You have to see the paintings that I have been doing.' At this time, she hadn't even seen my paintings. And when we got back from Puerto Rico she came over to see the paintings and she flipped, because it was the same animal, the same creature."

Leslie thinks that the dog entity has gone into people. With respect to just what the creature might be and how it could exist, Leslie has a number of beliefs. "Sometimes it's visible. It definitely lives on the lower astral. Sometimes it slips in but it also manifests and acts on the physical even when it is invisible. It definitely comes through in my paintings. It has been quite a long and involved story – at times quite frightening – leading me to investigate further as to who this entity might be. I thought it was Caribbean or African in origin."

Leslie's black dog theories

Leslie Merette believes that there is a connection between the black dog and snakes. Leslie says that on her trip to the Caribbean she and Julie encountered a "huge white sea serpent" that was five or six feet long. She described it as a fat, boa-like snake. "It followed us onto the shore," she reports. "It was there that we knew that something had been invoked." She had other "snake manifestations and snake dreams in relation to this [and] realized that the snake was the antidote, the protection."

"I think that the black dog is really rampant in the islands because there are no natural snakes. The natural enemy to the black dog is the snake: the natural dyad. In all of the Latin Caribbean islands, snakes have been eliminated. In the 1940s they brought in mongooses and eliminated the snake population of the island. The snake was the cure," opines Leslie. "The black dog is stronger when there is less to counter it." Her friend Julie told her that "where you find the poison, in the same area you will find what cures it – the antidote." Hence, Leslie's snake theories.

Whether we choose to agree or differ with Leslie Merette regarding her theories, and the context in which she places her encounter, one must remember that it is one thing to hear about such experiences and quite another to be in the midst of them. Leslie Merette vehemently proclaims, "When you've got it following you around, tormenting you, getting your dog hit by a car, trying to get into your motel room in the middle of the night – you need to work with it. You can't just explain it, you have to figure out what to do."

Mark Chorvinsky (1954-2005): FATE columnist and consulting editor, and founding editor of Strange *magazine.*

FATE February 1991

DOG AWFUL TRUTH ABOUT CRYPTIDS
Sean Casteel

They are the demon dogs from hell, the huge black canines with blazing eyes that haunt country lanes, and the phantom hounds that are regarded by some as Satan's personal minions.

In the new Global Communications/Conspiracy Journal book, Timothy Green Beckley's *Cryptid Creatures From Dark Domains: Dogmen, Devil Hounds, Phantom Canines and Real Werewolves*, the reader will indeed discover that there exists on the periphery of UFOs and aliens a shadowy realm of supernatural phenomena that includes many weird crypto-zoological monsters and creatures, none of which are housebroken and do not in any way, shape or form, make good domestic pets…demon dogs or hellhounds included!

Encounters with the oversized, flaming-eyed canines of torment and terror have been reported through the ages and have often been associated with subsequent death or other forms of tragedy. To hear such a creature howling in the night is to tread close to danger of many kinds.

Butch Witkowski stalks the dogman

In an interview conducted exclusively for this book, Butch Witkowski talks about his research into what he calls a "bipedal canine" who is frequently reported to appear in the state game lands of central Pennsylvania.

Witkowski began to study the paranormal after a UFO sighting he shared with several people went completely unacknowledged and unreported by the government and media. After he set up his own organization, called the UFO Research Center of Pennsylvania, with a gathering of like-minded UFO-believing individuals, he was surprised by the increasingly numerous reports of a doglike creature walking on two legs that were coming into the group.

"This is a real mystery to me," Witkowski said. "You know, I thought ufology was strange and hard to figure out, but it's kind of simple compared to this stuff."

The first report came to Witkowski in November of 2014 from a reliable witness – a retired pilot with 40 years of experience in both the military and with commercial airlines. Pilots are highly trained observers; it is a vital part of their job to accurately understand what their eyes behold. The pilot told Witkowski that he had been walking his two dogs in a familiar stretch of woods when the canines suddenly went berserk for no apparent reason. Next, the man beheld a tall, hairy, short-snouted "whatever the hell it was" that seemed totally oblivious to both him and his agitated hounds.

The man described the creature to Witkowski by saying, "If you would take Arnold Schwarzenegger and make him eight to ten feet tall – same body, massive chest, very thin waist, heavy-legged, muscular arms with hands."

The man added that he didn't see any ears, but he remarked that he hadn't really looked for ears. He had taken in the whole creature, which had a short snout similar to a bulldog or pug.

After struggling to get his dogs back in his vehicle, the man pulled a handgun out of the glovebox and walked into the woods again. He saw nothing. No broken branches or footprints.

The man subsequently returned to the scene – ignoring Witkowski's advice – with several heavily armed friends. Although the group saw nothing, they simultaneously began to feel deathly afraid, as though an invisible presence was making them fear for their lives. They literally walked backwards out of the area, too frightened to turn their backs on whatever was generating that collective terror.

Another Pennsylvania resident, a woman raised in a religious family, told Witkowski about seeing a similar creature standing at the edge of a pond near her home. The woman had been taught that if she were ever to see the devil, he would appear to her in animal form. "I truly believe," she told Witkowski, "that I was looking at the devil."

The creature is often called "demonic," according to Witkowski. He has also consulted Native Americans, including members of the Inuit and Cherokee tribes, who have told him they think it may be a creature called a "skinwalker," a shapeshifting spirit that could have gotten stuck somewhere between human and animal forms.

Whatever the creature is, it consistently terrifies those who encounter it.

"One thing that stands out in every report," Witkowski said, "is that the people feel 'This is not a good place to be right now. I need to get out of here or I'm going to die.' They have a fear that comes over them that just sets the impulse to fear and flee right into motion instantly, the minute they see it."

The Hollywood hellhound

Michele Lowe is a paranormal researcher who relates a fascinating personal experience in *Cryptid Creatures From Dark Domains*.

"When I was in my late teens, early twenties," she writes, "I used to hang out with my friends, like most people in Southern California. But I was a little weird. I loved all things Hollywood. I would recruit my friends all the time to go with me up to Hollywood to hang out."

Lowe first recounts a few Hollywood ghost stories, like hauntings by "Superman" actor George Reeves and Paul Bern, the husband of blonde bombshell actress Jean Harlow. Both Reeves and Bern committed suicide, and their troubled spirits can find no rest. Along with cruising the streets where ghosts allegedly materialized on a regular basis, Lowe and her friends were curious about seeing the house at 10050 Cielo Drive, where the Manson family had murdered pregnant actress Sharon Tate and several of her friends and peers.

They had to drive up a steep and narrow driveway before reaching the home's iron gate, which was where the first body was discovered the morning after the killings in 1969.

"The feeling of being so close to where such a horrific crime was committed," she continues, "was very sobering. The atmosphere was very heavy there, and it just didn't feel right. So we left."

Lowe writes that they decided to explore some of the other Hollywood neighborhoods, consoled by the bright lights and a more cheerful ambience.

It was then that a giant black dog came charging at the car.

"It was huge," she recalled, "and had this very thick black fur. The dog's back and head easily came up to the window of the car."

Lowe and a female friend screamed in panic while Cuz Dave, the driver, hit the gas pedal. Even when the car reached 35 mph, the dog had no problem keeping up the pace.

"It was literally right next to the car," Lowe writes, "looking at us as if it was out to kill! It was barking violently as we tried to drive away in sheer terror. We drove about a mile or so before Dave finally slowed down and turned into another neighborhood so we could calm down and regroup. Just as we were starting to calm down, the giant black dog literally appeared out of nowhere and came charging at the car.

"We again screamed and Dave took off again. We could not believe this was happening. There was no way that dog could have kept up with us when Dave took off out of that last neighborhood over a mile away! We quickly got out of that neighborhood and again lost the crazed dog. This time, though, we didn't stop. We went straight home."

Many readers, according to Lowe, might mistakenly think the young people were only dealing with someone's pet. But she counters that assumption, saying she had never seen a dog so enormous. Its speed was also mind blowing, since it ran right next to the car without straining to keep up.

"It was clear the dog could have run even faster if it wanted to," Lowe writes. "And then there is the fact that we drove off as fast as we could a mile or more away to another neighborhood and were there only a couple of minutes when, literally out of nowhere, the dog appeared again and started charging us at full speed. How could it even find us again? Even though we didn't understand it then, we still knew that what happened was not normal."

Over the ensuing years, Lowe began to study the paranormal in a quest for answers to the brush with the supernatural she and her friends had shared.

"Knowing what I know now," she reasons, "I believe that what we encountered was a hellhound. I had heard of them before but didn't know what they were. So I did some research and this is what I found: A hellhound is a supernatural dog, usually very large with thick black fur. They are unnaturally strong and fast and have red eyes. Sometimes the eyes are yellow. It is said that they are assigned to guard the entrance to the home of the dead, like graveyards or burial grounds. They also have other duties to do with the afterlife, like hunting down lost souls. They can also be an omen of death."

Nick Redfen struggles with the fiery hounds—and a UFO connection

Cryptid Creatures From Dark Domains also features the work of Nick Redfern, one of the most visible faces in the field of paranormal research. Redfern has testified that his bedroom was once "invaded" by a werewolf-type creature which crept closer and closer to where he was sleeping and then suddenly vanished. Redfern begins his chapter with a genuinely frightening story, told in second person, of a hapless traveler encountering a hellhound and fleeing for his life. One is then informed that the story was not a work of fiction, but actually happened in 1997 in a small English village called Ranton.

"But what are these infernal creatures?" Redfern asks. "Are they legend, reality, or both? And how, and under what circumstances, did they inspire the most famous, cherished and loved Sherlock Holmes story of all time? Published in 1902, Conan Doyle's *The Hound of the Baskervilles* tells the memorable and atmosphere-filled saga of the noted and wealthy Baskerville family that has called Dartmoor, Devonshire, England, its home for centuries. Dartmoor is filled with supernatural tales of terror, horror and intrigue – but leading them all is the legend of the terrible hound that haunts the Baskervilles."

Conan Doyle took the lead from all-too-real supernatural occurrences of the paranormal hound on Dartmoor. He also relied on stories about a real-life resident of Devonshire County named Richard Cabell, a monstrously evil squire who may have sold his soul to the devil himself for personal gain. When Cabell died in 1677, presumably into the embrace of his fork-tailed, horned master, a pack of supernatural hounds materialized on the old moors and raced for Cabell's tomb, where they howled ominously all night long and struck cold fear into the locals.

"Thus, the story began to develop in Conan Doyle's mind and imagination," Redfern continues. "He moved the location of the old hall to Dartmoor and changed Richard Cabell to the evil Hugo Baskerville. In the process, literary history was made and *The Hound of the Baskervilles* was born. But there is one important factor to remember: Conan Doyle did not invent Britain's fiery-eyed hounds. He merely brought them to the attention of the public in spectacularly entertaining, fictional style."

For those looking for a possible link to the UFO phenomenon, one does not have to travel through a black hole to find what appears to be a very positive connection.

It is at this point that Redfern begins to chronicle several instances of people encountering the real thing, and in more recent times than one might think. For example, there is the story of Nigel Lea, who in the early weeks of 1972 was driving across the Cannock Chase woods that dominate much of Staffordshire when he saw a strange ball of glowing blue light that seemingly came out of nowhere and slammed violently into the ground some short distance ahead of him before releasing a torrent of bright, fiery sparks. As he slowly approached the area where the light had fallen, he was both shocked and horrified to see looming before him "the biggest bloody dog I have ever seen in my life."

"Very muscular, and utterly black in color," Redfern goes on, "with a pair of large, pointed ears and huge thick paws, the creature seemed to positively ooze both extreme menace and overpowering negativity, and had a crazed, staring look in its yellow-tinged eyes. For 20 or 30 seconds, both man and beast alike squared off against each other in classic stalemate fashion, after which the animal both slowly and carefully headed for the darkness and the camouflage of the tall surrounding trees, not even once taking its penetrating eyes off of the petrified driver as it did so."

Somewhat ominously, two or three weeks later, a close friend of Lea's from back in his childhood days was killed in a horrific industrial accident in a West Midlands town. Today, after having deeply studied – almost to the point of obsession – the history of British Black Dog lore and the creature's associations with both deep tragedy and death, Lea believes his strange encounter was directly connected.

Black Shuck and the Shug Monkey in Rendlesham Forest

According to Redfern, perhaps the most famous of all of the phantom hounds of old Britain are those that are said to have frequented, and in some cases still frequent, the ancient roads and pathways of Norfolk, Essex, Suffolk and Sussex. Their various names include Black Shuck, the Shug Monkey and the Shock. The Shuck and the Shock are classic black dogs, whereas the Shug Monkey is described as being a combination of spectral monkey and immense hound.

"Even their very names have intriguing origins," Redfern writes. "While some researchers consider the possibility that all of the appellations had their origins in the word 'Shucky,' an ancient east coast term meaning 'shaggy,' others suggest a far more sinister theory, namely that Shock, Shuck and Shug are all based upon the Anglo-Saxon 'scucca,' meaning 'demon,' a most apt description for sure."

In the winter of 1983, a couple in their twenties, Paul and Jayne Jennings, encountered a black dog in Rendlesham Forest, home to Britain's most famous UFO encounter, the December 1980 event in which numerous personnel from the nearby Royal Air Force Bentwaters military base encountered a UFO in the woods. Like Nigel Lea's witnessing a glowing blue light before his face-to-face meeting with a black dog, the close proximity of the military's UFO incident creates a tenuous connection between both phenomena.

The Jenningses were walking along a trail in the Rendlesham Forest when, according to Redfern, they saw what Jayne described as a "big black dog that kept appearing and disappearing." When Redfern asked her to elaborate, she explained that on rounding a bend on the path they came face to face with the dog, which was a huge creature whose head was unmistakably that of a large hound while the body, strangely, was more feline in nature.

The dog was not aggressive, and seemed to have a mournful expression on its face. But the Jennings were shocked when it vanished in the blink of an eye. They were even more shocked when a moment later it reappeared and proceeded to "flicker on and off" four or five times before vanishing permanently. After the dog's disappearance, the air was filled with a strange smell that resembled "burning metal." Could it be the fires of hell, to which the mournful-looking dog was dispiritedly returning? And what of the possible Rendlesham connection? Are the weird goings-on there proof that this might be what John Keel once determined to be a "window area" to another dimension?

The hounds in mythology

Further along in his chapter, Redfern tells the story of the Wild Hunt and even wilder hounds. He quotes the famed crypto-zoologist Jon Downes: "Belief in the Wild Hunt is found not only in Britain but also on the Continent, and the basic idea is the same in all variations: a phantasmal leader and his men accompanied by hounds who 'fly' through the night in pursuit of something. What they are pursuing is not clear; although Norse legend has various objects such as a visionary boar or wild horse, and even magical maidens known as Moss Maidens.

"Greek myth has Hecate roaming the Earth on moonless nights with a pack of ghostly, howling dogs and the phenomenon has also been reported from Germany, where, according to folklore, the procession includes the souls of unbaptized babies in the train of 'Frau Bertha,' who sometimes accompanied the wild huntsman."

(The mythic apparition of the Wild Hunt is said to resemble, and may have inspired, a well-known Country and Western song called "Ghost Riders in the Sky," in which a band of ghostly cowboys is condemned forever to chase a herd of cattle across the sky yet never actually catch them. The song has been recorded by the likes of Johnny Cash, Gene Autry, Bing Crosby and Peggy Lee, as well as a later rock version by The Outlaws.)

Downes explains that the hounds are universally believed to be portents of war, death and disaster, and an unfortunate traveler who heard one would fling himself face downward to the ground to avoid seeing the beast. The Devil's hunting pack, and the related phenomenon of the Devil Dogs, have been reported on more occasions during years of warfare than at any other time.

Black dogs from colonial times to the present

Fortean blogger Andrew Gable ably adds a history of black dog hauntings in the United States.

"Legends of black dogs and phantom hounds," Gable writes, "are widespread throughout the Chesapeake Bay region, which was one of the earliest areas settled by the English. The tales of British black dogs were combined with werewolf traditions and typical ghost stories, as well as possibly with crypto-zoological sightings of weird creatures, to create traditions that are like the British ones, and yet unlike them at the same time."

One of the interesting stories Gable relates concerns a phantom hound named "Snarly Yow" who haunted a section of the National Pike near Turner's Gap in Frederick County, Maryland. Gable references an 1882 book by Madeleine V. Dahlgren called South Mountain Magic in which no less than a dozen sightings of the beast are recorded.

A man named Daniel Mesick testified that his father kicked at a huge dog near Dame's Quarter and his foot passed directly through it. Sticks, rocks and even bullets were said to pass right through the "animal." Other accounts have it that the dog left physical traces and frightened horses so much they threw their riders.

"A staple of Frederick County legendry for years," Gable writes, "the Yow was seen in 1962 near Zittlestown. In this instance, it was headless, white and dragged a chain along behind it."

There is a phantom dog called the Fence Rail Dog, an enormous hound nearly 10 feet long, which haunts a stretch of Route 12 near Frederica in Delaware. The dog appears in the wake of automobile accidents on the road. Gable points out that folklore from around the globe speaks of dogs as a kind of psycho-pomp – or spirits which guide the dead to the afterlife – and that the Fence Rail Dog's appearance in the wake of death may be an example of this.

Gable also recounts the folklore concerning an outlaw named Silas Werninger, who was cornered in his home but committed suicide rather than be taken by his pursuers. He was buried in the forest near his home, and after his death a large black wolf emerged from the grove and menaced townspeople. A witch advised the people to dig up the outlaw's remains and bury them in consecrated ground to dispel the phantasmal wolf.

Gable says the source of the folklore is the real-life story of a Pennsylvania outlaw named William Etlinger, who did indeed kill himself after taking his wife and children hostage. His cabin was burnt to the ground by authorities trying to flush him out. It is said that the cabin sometimes reappears on its burnt foundations and that the outlaw's body was moved after it was felt a black wolf familiar in the area may have been feeding on the corpse. Even suicidal outlaws deserve better. There is more to the story Gable tells than is recorded here, but let's leave that to readers of the actual book, eh?

Demon dogs and the MIB?

Claudia Cunningham, nicknamed "The MIB Lady," relates the story of how she and Timothy Green Beckley visit the grave of Charles Fort in Albany Rural Cemetery, near the state capitol of New York. Cunningham says that perhaps the site where Fort and his entire family are entombed is a fitting place for dastardly black hounds and phantom dogs from hell to be seen since Fort collected such beastly stories throughout his writing career and placed them in the volumes that make up *The Complete Works of Charles Fort*.

While Cunningham and Beckley failed to sight any phantom dogs of their own, their story still makes for a lively break in the action, to include some local Men-In-Black stories that center around the cemetery just outside Albany. In addition to being the place where Charles Fort is buried, the graveyard is the resting spot of a president of the United States, Chester Arthur. Is it any wonder haunting hounds, the MIB and other strange incidents raise their heads up from the etheric there from time to time?

Cunningham then goes on to record several late 19th and early 20th century stories from Fort's research concerning the mysterious slayers of sheep in the UK. In one case in England, the police were unable to explain how the sheep had died since it was not possible for the killer to have been a mere dog.

"Dogs are not vampires," said Sergeant Carter of the Gloucestershire Police, "and do not suck the blood of a sheep and leave the flesh almost untouched."

A few weeks later, a newspaper report declared that the "marauder" had been shot and was said to be a large black dog, which Cunningham claims was an early example of convenient "debunking," a pattern repeated throughout the history of the subject of demon dogs by the newspapers of the time. It appears that even in Fort's time, a media cover-up of the paranormal was firmly in place.

Swartz, Steiger, and Kern stare down the werewolves

Also included in *Cryptid Creatures From Dark Domains* is a chapter by paranormal researcher extraordinaire Tim Swartz, who writes about the folklore of his native Indiana. In the early 18th century, French fur trappers making their way south from Canada encountered their own version of the canine nightmare called the *loup-garou*, a supernatural threat more frightening than any wild and predatory "earthly" wolf.

The *loup-garou* often appeared as a monstrous wolf but could also shapeshift into a cow, horse, or any other animal. The creatures were also said to have mental powers; under their spell, a human victim became an enraged animal that roamed at night through the fields and forests. During the day, the unfortunate reverted to his human form but was sickly and fearful to tell of his predicament. People at the time believed that such was the fate of those who violated the rules of the Catholic observance of Lent.

Swartz is also a scholar of cinema and provides several pages of background and poster art from movies about werewolves.

Not to be outdone, legendary paranormal writer Brad Steiger offers his chapter, called "The Terrible Hungers of Real-Life Vampires, Werewolves and Ghouls." The title alone should whet your appetite for Steiger's fascinating historical study of monstrous crimes committed before the advent of modern psychiatry, which taught us to attribute such things to simple human sadism and sexual perversion. In times past, Steiger writes, evil spirits got the blame, but perhaps we moderns should instead search "the wasteland of man's subconscious."

Then, finally, there is William Kern's short story, "The Man Who Fell From a Clear Blue Sky." Kern is a sort of jack-of-all-trades; he writes both fiction and nonfiction, as well as working as a graphic artist and layout designer, to include his designing efforts on *Cryptid Creatures From Dark Domains*. Kern's short story revolves around the phenomenon of "changelings," specifically human/wolf changelings, which are called "hulfs," we learn.

The reader will most likely agree that the new book covers the subject of supernatural canines very thoroughly, does it not? To which we can only add, "We double-dog dare you to take a walk on the wild side and read *Cryptid Creatures From Dark Domains*."

Suggested reading:

- *Cryptid Creatures from Dark Domains: Dogmen, Devil Hounds, Phantom Canines And Real Werewolves.*
- *America's Strange and Supernatural History: Includes Prophecies Of The Presidents.*
- *It's Raining Cats and Dogs: Ghostly Pets, Phantom Felines and Haunted Hounds.*

Sean Casteel: Author and writer on ufology, cryptids and related topics.

FATE #730 2017

Appendix
A Gazeteer of Werewolves and Their Kin
Rosemary Ellen Guiley

A selection of werewolves and related man-beasts from international lore.

buda

In ancient Abbyssinian lore, certain potters or ironworkers had the power to shapeshift into budas, which were werewolves and other ravenous beasts such as hyenas. Budas possessed the malevolent power of the evil eye, the ability to harm or kill by looking. Budas did their shapeshifting only on one day of the year. They also wore peculiar earrings, which sometimes were found in the ears of trapped hyenas. Herodotus, a Greek historian of the 5th century BCE, said he did not believe the stories he heard about werewolf budas.

liderc

In Hungarian lore, the liderc is a supernatural entity with associations to the vampire, witch, werewolf, nightmare hag, incubus and succubus. The liderc can be of human or demonic origins, and can take on an animal form.

One type of liderc, the mit-make, is a helping spirit similar to the familiar of a witch. The mit-make lives in houses and performs endless chores. It takes the form of a chicken without feathers, appearing on its own or else hatched from an egg that is carried in the armpit. The mit-make can shapeshift to human form.

The mit-make literally helps its master to death. It works so fast and efficiently that it pesters its master for more and more. If not given sufficient work, it destroys its master. Once in a house it is extremely difficult to dislodge. The only way to prevent it from becoming destructive is to give it impossible tasks, like carrying water or sand in a sieve. In some cases, the it can be stuffed into a hole in a tree trunk.

Other liderc are dark and demonic, and create nightmares. A dead person who becomes a liderc lives as a night vampire.

The liderc also has sexual associations, supported by the belief that the double of another creature can be summoned by intense desire. Liderc lovers are really devil lovers whose intense and unrelenting affections cause their victims to waste away. They like to prey upon people whose lovers or spouses have been absent too long or who have died.

The incubus/succubus liderc comes down the chimney in the form of a flame or star. When it shapeshifts to human form it has one leg like a goose, which gives away its true identity. Its entry can be prevented by taking a trousers belt or cord and securing the bedroom door with it. If a liderc has already gained entry to a house, it can be banished by hiding its human boot.

lobishomen

The lobishomen is a predatory entity in Brazilian and Portuguese folklore that has both vampire and werewolf characteristics. Like the jaracacas, a Brazilian vampire in the shape of a snake, the lobishomen preys upon nursing mothers, sucking only enough blood to satisfy itself without killing. The bite turns women into nymphomaniacs.

In some Portuguese stories, the lobishomen is more of a werewolf creature that sucks the blood of children. It appears as a small, humpbacked creature that has hairy, stumpy legs and a pale face with white lips and snaggly black teeth. Its skin is yellow.

The lobishomen is smart and crafty, but it gets drunk quite easily. It can be trapped by leaving out glasses of wine. After it becomes inebriated, it can be overpowered and killed, preferably by stabbing or crucifixion on a tree. The corpse is burned.

A knife or sword used for killing a lobishomen must be destroyed. In some beliefs, however, the weapon acquires a magical power and serves as a protection to keep evil beings away.

louleerou

In French lore, the louleerou is a certain kind of man, especially a bastard, who is compelled to transform into a diabolical beast at the full moon.

The transformation always takes place at night. In a fit, the man dashes out a window and plunges into a well. He emerges with a goatskin that the devil has given him, and dons it. Transformed, he runs about the countryside on all fours, attacking and devouring dogs that he finds. At dawn he takes off his goatskin and returns home.

The louleerou often becomes sick from the dogs he has eaten, and vomits undigested paws.

If killed or wounded while in the loulerou state, the beast will return instantly to his human form at the first spilling of his blood. Thus recognized, he brings great shame upon his family.

loup-garou (also rougarou)
In French lore, the loup-garou is a man or woman who can transform into a wolf at will and retain the full faculties of a human. If wounded by a person, the loup-garou returns to its own human form, and the victim must become a loup-garou for 101 days. If they talk about what happened to them, they remain a loup-garou. Loup-garou stories often involve the revenge of jealous lovers.

oborot
The oborot is a Russian werewolf; the term means "one transformed." A person can magically transform himself into an oborot. First, he must go into a forest and find a tree that has been cut down. He stabs the tree with a copper knife and walks around the tree, repeating an incantation:

> On the sea, on the ocean, on the island, on Bujan,
> On the empty pasture gleams the moon, on an ashstock lying
> In a green wood, in a gloomy vale.
> Toward the stock wandereth a shaggy wolf,
> Horned cattle seeking for his sharp white fangs;
> But the wolf enters not the forest,
> But the wolf dives not into the shadowy vale,
> Moon, moon, gold-horned moon,
> Check the flight of bullets, blunt the hunters' knives,
> Break the shepherds' cudgels,
> Cast wild fear upon all cattle,
> On men, on all creeping things,

That they may not catch the grey wolf,
That they may not rend his warm skin!
My word is binding, more binding than sleep,
More binding than the promise of a hero!

The person then springs over the tree three times. He will be transformed into a wolf, and can run off into the forest.

ruvanush

In the lore of Gypsies, ruvanush is a Romany term for "wolf-man," from *ruv* "wolf" and *manush* "man." A ruvanush can be created by vampiric witches who suck the blood of men born during the waxing moon. A victim becomes a fierce werewolf by night. Even after resuming his human form at dawn, the ruvanush can consume only raw flesh and blood.

A witch can also be a ruvanush, as illustrated in the account of a 19th-century case of a poor Hungarian Gypsy fiddler named Kropan, who lived with his wife in Toresz in northern Hungary. Kropan became aware that his wife was slipping out of the house at night. He suspected her of carrying on an affair, and so he secretly watched her. She would wait until she thought he was asleep and then leave. But she was not out dallying with a lover. To Kropan's horror, she would return at dawn in the form of a wolf and change back into her human shape. She brought with her livestock she had killed, which she proceeded to cook for her husband.

Kropan said nothing. His earnings barely bought them bread, so he was grateful for the selection of fine meats, including lamb, beef, pork and chicken. The couple had so much meat that he started selling it in a nearby town, and grew rich in profits. He opened an inn that sold inexpensive dishes, and attracted even more business.

Eventually the wolfish ravages of the wife aroused suspicion among the villagers. Exposed, both Kropan and his wife were exorcized by a priest. When sprinkled with holy water, the wife shrieked as though she had been plunged into boiling oil. She disappeared. The angry mob turned on Kropan and killed him. Two peasants held to be the ringleaders of the murder were convicted and imprisoned for six years. They were released in 1881.

vilkacis (vilkatas, vilkatis)
A vilkacis ("wolf's eyes") is a male werewolf in Latvian and Lithuanian lore. A female version is called the vilkatas. Transformation takes place both in physical ways and in astral, spirit ways. The male vilkacis shapeshifts into a wolf in various ways:

- During sleep as a form of astral projection called "running with the wolf"
- Being cursed
- Committing sins
- Donning wolf skins and reciting charms
- Going out on the night of a full moon, finding a tree whose top branches have grown into the ground and formed an arch, and standing in the arch

The female vilkatas transforms by taking off her clothes and hiding them. If the clothing is found and touched, the women cannot return to her normal form for a period of years, anywhere from one to nine. During that time, she may run around her home in circles, trying to make contact with her husband and children.

The vilkacis hunts for food in the forests, but usually stays close to its human home. As in other werewolf lore, of the vilkacis is wounded while in wolf form, the same wound appears on the human body. If the wolf is killed, then the human dies, too.

German invaders and landlords were portrayed in the form of the vilkacis. Other stories tell of servants turning into werewolves and attacking livestock – perhaps a way of expressing anger toward foreign masters.

vilkodlak
This is a medieval term in Bohemia for werewolf.

volkolak
In West Slavic lore, the volkolak is a werewolf. A folk tale tells about a volkolak who has nine daughters, and grows weary of supporting them all. He goes out into the forest to chop wood. His daughters come one by one, staring with the oldest, to bring him food. He throws them into a pit, kills them, and roasts their heads.

The youngest – and most beautiful – daughter knows he is a werewolf. She is the last to arrive, and enquires about her sisters. He leads her to the pit and tells her to undress, for she is about to die. The girl asks her father to turn around while she undresses. She seizes the moment and pushes him into the pit, but he climbs out and chases her, howling in rage. She throws her kerchief behind her and says he cannot catch her until he tears the kerchief to pieces, unravels them, spins them, weaves them and stitches them anew. This the werewolf does in half an hour.

The chase resumes. The girl casts off her skirt, dress, vest and blouse, and the werewolf does the same to them as he did to the kerchief. Finally the girl hides herself in a small haystack. The werewolf tears all the haystacks up but cannot find his daughter. He goes away howling in a furious rage.

Three days later a king comes along, hunting in the forest. His dog finds the girl, and the king marries her. Her one condition is that no beggar ever be allowed to spend the night in their castle. They have two sons and are very happy.

Several years later, the werewolf comes to the castle disguised as a beggar, and convinces the staff to let him inside to sleep under a broom. In the middle of the night, he slits the throats of the sons with his daughter's knife, which he lays upon them. He escapes.

The king drives away his wife, but lets her bind the necks of his sons. She wanders until she finds a hermit, who directs her to a lizard who has a curative herb in its mouth. With this she restores the dead sons to life. The king takes her back.

Once again the werewolf comes to the castle and tries to get in for the night. He is recognized by the servants and taken before the king. He confesses to slaying the sons. The king has the werewolf bound to a wagon and pushed over a cliff into the sea. The werewolf breaks his neck and perishes. The king, his wife and sons live happily ever after.

vlokoslak
This Serbian is applied to both vampires and werewolves. The werewolves like to hold gatherings in winter. They meet in the woods and hang their wolfskins on trees. If anyone finds the skins and burns them, the werewolves will be disenchanted.

vrykolakas (vrykolacas)

The most common Greek term for vampire, "vrykolakas," is derived from a Bulgarian term, varkolak, meaning "werewolf." The vrykolakas is a corpse possessed by a demon, who causes it to return to the living to wreak horror and destruction. The word "vampire" was not known in Greece, but over time the vrykolakas became associated with the European versions of the vampire. Belief in vrykolakes (plural) was particularly strong from the 17th to 20th centuries.

The vrykolakas also has associations with the nightmare hag, for it sits on the chests of sleeping people and suffocates them.

A second type of vrykolakas is more like a werewolf: a living sorcerer who, on moonlit nights, goes into a form of sleepwalking and is seized with a bloodlust, causing it to hunt down humans and animals and tear them to pieces. If a person is a werewolf in life, they will become a vryolakas vampire after death. Other ways to become a vrykolakas vampire are to practice witchcraft and sorcery, and to eat the meat of sheep killed by a werewolf.

vukodlak

The vukodlak is a Serbo-Croatian vampire. The name "vukodlak" means "wolf's hair," and most often refers to a male. The vukodlak has been associated with werewolves in the English sense of the word, which some scholars say is not accurate.

In its earliest form, the vukodlak was associated with eclipses as an eater of the sun and moon. The earliest description of a vukodlak dates to a Serbian account of 1262, which states, "the pursuers of the clouds were called vukodlaci by the peasants. If the moon or the sun is extinguished, they say that the vukodlaci have devoured the moon or the sun. But all this is fables and lies."

Bulgarian and Macedonian folklore texts describe the vukodlak as an imaginary evil spirit incarnated from the of a murdered person. In other lore, a child born feet first or with teeth will become a vudkolak. A man can become a vudkolak by being transformed by a sorcerer through magical power, especially when he is on his way to his wedding. If so transformed, he will run about the village in the form of a wolf, casting plaintive looks about for help, but he will remain in wolf form until the spell is undone by the same sorcerer who cast it.

The vudkolak sleeps in the grave with its eyes open. It hair and nails grow to excessive lengths. When the moon is full, it leaves the grave and attacks men to drink their blood.

wawkalak

The wawalak is a White Russian werewolf that has been cursed by the devil. The wawkalak is a man who incurs the wrath of the devil, and is punished by being transformed into a wolf and sent among his relations. The wakalak is recognized by his family, who feeds him and takes care of him. He has a gentle disposition and wreaks no havoc, and even displays his affection by licking the hands of his benefactors. But the wakalak is doomed to be driven from village to village by his own need for change. Stories of the wakalak illustrate the dangers of angering the devil.

About FATE Magazine

Six decades before the AMC's *Walking Dead*, SyFy's *Paranormal Witness*, late-night radio's *Coast to Coast AM*, and countless websites, blogs, books, and movies began captivating audiences with true tales of the paranormal – there was FATE – a first-of-its-kind publication dedicated to in-depth coverage of mysterious and unexplained phenomena.

FATE was a true journalistic pioneer, covering issues like electronic voice phenomena, cattle mutilations, life on Mars, telepathic communication with animals, and UFOs at a time when discussing such things was neither hip nor trendy. Today FATE enjoys a rare longevity achieved by only a select few U.S. periodicals.

Where it all began: The birth of the modern UFO era

The year was 1948. The Cold War was in its infancy, and the Space Age was still a dream...but across the nation and around the world, people observed strange objects flying through the skies.

Two Chicago-based magazine editors, Raymond A. Palmer and Curtis B. Fuller, took a close look at the public's fascination with flying saucers and saw the opportunity of a lifetime. With help from connections in the worlds of science fiction and alternative spirituality, they launched a new magazine dedicated to the objective exploration of the world's mysteries. They gave their "cosmic reporter" the name FATE.

FATE's first issue, published in Spring 1948, featured as its cover story the first-hand report of pilot Kenneth Arnold on his UFO sighting of the previous year, an event widely recognized by UFO historians as the birth of the modern UFO era.

FATE's role in creating a new genre: The paranormal

Other topics covered in this and subsequent issues included vanished civilizations, communication with spirits, synchronicity, exotic religions, monsters and giants, out-of-place artifacts, and phenomena too bizarre for categorization. This mix of subjects set a template that the magazine would follow for six decades and counting. In many ways, FATE magazine created the genre that is now known as "the paranormal."

Palmer and Fuller's judgment of FATE's potential proved correct, and as demand for the magazine grew its publication frequency increased quickly from quarterly to bimonthly to monthly. Palmer sold his share of the magazine in the late 1950s, and Fuller brought his wife Mary aboard to help run the growing business.

FATE's success spawned scores of imitators over the years, but none lasted very long. Through the decades FATE kept going, doggedly promoting the validity of paranormal studies but unafraid to reveal major events as hoaxes or frauds when it was warranted. Among the famous cases debunked by FATE were the Philadelphia Experiment, and the book and movie versions of the Amityville Horror.

Relevant today

So how does FATE still stay relevant after all this time? Especially in a fast-paced, high-tech world that is often short on attention span and long on cynicism, how does a magazine like FATE continue to thrive? Editor-in-Chief Phyllis Galde says, "FATE allows readers to think for themselves by providing them with stories that mainstream publications don't dare touch. The truth is, reality does not conform to the neat and tidy box that many people would like to wedge it into. Our world is a bizarre and wondrous place and our universe is filled with mystery – it is teeming with the unknown. People are longing for something more than the mundane transactions of everyday existence. FATE feeds the soul's appetite for the enigmatic, the esoteric, and the extraordinary."

Subscribe to FATE

FATE is published in intervals throughout the year in a popular digest size. Join the family of subscribers by visiting the FATE website at www.fatemag.com!

About Rosemary Ellen Guiley

Rosemary Ellen Guiley, executive editor of FATE magazine, is a leading expert in the metaphysical and paranormal fields, with more than 65 books published on a wide range of paranormal, spiritual, and mystical topics, including nine single-volume encyclopedias and reference works, translated into 15 languages. Her work focuses on interdimensional entity contact experiences of all kinds (spirit, alien, creature), the afterlife and spirit communications, contact with extraterrestrials, aliens and nonhuman intelligent beings, problem hauntings, spirit and entity attachments, psychic skills, dreamwork for well-being, spiritual growth and development, angels, past and parallel lives, and investigation of unusual paranormal activity. She has worked full-time as an investigator, researcher, author, and presenter since 1983, and spends a great deal of time in the field doing original research.

Rosemary is president and owner of Visionary Living, Inc., a publishing and media company. She hosts a weekly radio show, *Strange Dimensions,* on the KGRA digital broadcast network, Wednesdays from 8-10 PM Eastern. She makes numerous appearances on radio and in documentaries, docu-dramas and television shows.

In addition, she is a board director of the Foundation for Research into Extraterrestrial Encounters (FREE), a scientific organization to educate, support, and research the field of ET and entity contact and abduction experiences, and of the Academy for Spiritual and Consciousness Studies. She is a past board member of the International Association for the Study of Dreams.

A personal note from Rosemary

I have been privileged to be part of the FATE family since 1991-92. Dennis Stillings, the publisher of *Artifex* magazine, brought me to the Minneapolis area to give a lecture on vampires – my book *Vampires Among Us* had just been published. In the audience were Phyllis Galde and David Godwin, editors of FATE. They invited me to contribute to FATE, and a lasting friendship was struck.

I started as a columnist for FATE; my column was called "Gateways." I joined the prestigious company of other FATE columnists and regulars, among them John A. Keel, Mark Chorvinsky, Loyd Auerbach, Antonio Huneeus, and Loren Coleman.

Over the course of time, FATE went through changes. Phyllis and David departed to set up their own publishing company, Galde Press. In the early 2000s, they purchased FATE from Llewellyn. David passed in 2012, and FATE remains under Phyllis's ownership. The economic upheavals in publishing, combined with rapid changes in the delivery of information, have impacted FATE. One a monthly magazine, it is now is published several times a year – still delivering the same varied and insightful content.

I went from columnist to consulting editor, and in 2016 became executive editor, taking on more editing responsibilities. Phyllis and I entered into a partnership to bring you a series of books on the best from the archives of FATE on timeless topics of ongoing interest. FATE has thousands of excellent articles in its vaults, written by the best of the best, and I am pleased to make them available again.

Made in the USA
Las Vegas, NV
16 January 2021